For Rita and Lee Rouner
with esteem and gratitude
for friendship over the years
from
John Woolverton

October 1995

Studies in Anglican History

Series Editor
Peter W. Williams, Miami University

Sponsored by the Historical Society of the Episcopal Church

The Education of Phillips Brooks

THE EDUCATION OF
Phillips Brooks

John F. Woolverton

University of Illinois Press
Urbana & Chicago

Publication of this work has been supported by a grant
from the Historical Society of the Episcopal Church.

This book is printed on acid-free paper.

Frontispiece: Phillips Brooks in 1859, the year he graduated from the
Virginia Episcopal Theological Seminary (bMS AM 1594.1, 635, box
17). Reproduced by permission of the Houghton Library, Harvard
University.

Library of Congress Cataloging-in-Publication Data

Woolverton, John Frederick, 1926–
The education of Phillips Brooks / John F. Woolverton.
p.   cm. — (Studies in Anglican history)
Includes bibliographical references and index.
ISBN 0-252-02186-X (alk. paper)
1. Brooks, Phillips, 1835–1893. 2. Episcopal Church—
Massachusetts—Bishops—Education—History—19th century.
3. Anglican Communion—Massachusetts—Bishops—Education
History—19th century. 4. Massachusetts—Church history—19th
century. I. Title. II. Series.
BX5995.B8W66   1995
283'.092—dc20
[B]   95-1881
                                                CIP

*For the people of Trinity Church, Portland, Maine
with gratitude and affection*

Series Editor's Preface

Peter W. Williams

"Studies in Anglican History" is a series of scholarly mono-
graphs sponsored by the Historical Society of the Episcopal Church
and published by the University of Illinois Press. It is intended to bring
the best of contemporary international scholarship on the history of
the entire Anglican Communion, including the Church of England and
the Episcopal church in the United States, to a broader readership.

John Woolverton, longtime editor of *Anglican and Episcopal History*, addresses in *The Education of Phillips Brooks* the early intellectual and religious development of one of the best-known "Princes
of the Pulpit" of Victorian America. Little has been published about
Brooks since Raymond Albright's biography of 1961, and much that
has been written has been either excessively critical or hagiographic.
Woolverton steers a more balanced course, arguing that Brooks was
not simply a Gilded Age urban icon or a sterling example of Victorian manhood but a gifted Protestant clergyman nurtured in an atmosphere of serious religious thought. Drawing on many previously
neglected archival sources, Woolverton sketches the formative stages
of Brooks's career as he sought a religious and cultural ideal in a time
of national crisis and found that ideal in the "perfect manhood" of
Jesus Christ. The result is a fresh look at Brooks, one that does not
claim him as a major theologian but adds considerable nuance to
earlier one-sided interpretations of this highly public man who embodied the spirit of his age's public religion.

Contents

Preface

I remember being in a small class one day when I was a student at the Virginia Theological Seminary. The class was led by a young professor named William A. Clebsch who went on to become chairman of the Department of Religion at Stanford University. In his characteristic manner, Clebsch made a provocative remark designed to induce the class to think for itself and in the process to bring it alive. I cannot recall what the topic was, but I remember the reaction of one shocked student who said, "But you wouldn't tell that to the laity!" Clebsch gleefully replied, "I am."

Thereafter I began to ponder the whole matter of clericalism and years later began research for a book on the laity of the Episcopal church. One of the categories of layperson, thought I, should be theological students. I hit upon Phillips Brooks. In the process of reading Brooks's papers at the Houghton Library at Harvard University, I came to two conclusions: (1) I could not, unlike Clebsch, possibly get away with calling Brooks a layman. No one would allow it. (2) As is often the case, the more I read, the more interested I became in Brooks and the years of his growth to adulthood, the 1850s. The result was a scholarly detour to complete a study of young Phillips Brooks.

The Education of Phillips Brooks is very much a monograph—by which I mean that there is a great deal more to be said about him by church historians, even about his early years. It is my hope that this study will inspire others to deal with his life and thought and that a full edition of his works, suitably edited, may yet appear.

I would like to thank the staffs of the following institutions who aided me in my research: Houghton Library at Harvard University, the Massachusetts Historical Society, and the New England Historic Genealogical Society. I am grateful to Mitzi Jarrett Budde of the Bishop Payne Library at Virginia Theological Seminary for sending me numerous volumes by Brooks as well as works on the 1850s. I wish also to thank the faculty of the Episcopal Divinity School in Cambridge, Massachusetts, for making me a visiting scholar with the many library privileges at Harvard and elsewhere that went with that opportunity. Peter Williams and his able referees helped me more than I can say in changing, enlarging, and refining the original manuscript. Finally, a special word of thanks to my friend Joseph Conforti, director of New England studies at the University of Southern Maine, for early and helpful encouragement. The results, for good or ill, are completely mine.

Finally, I want to thank my wife, Maggie, for her support and advice at a time when she herself was in the midst of writing and editing her mother's letters from Moscow during World War I and the Russian Revolution of 1917–18.

Introduction

Phillips Brooks died on Monday, 23 January 1893, at the age of fifty-seven.[1] On the day of his funeral, 26 January, Boston came to a virtual standstill. "The Boston Stock Exchange and many of the business houses of the city closed from 11 o'clock until 2," reported the *New York Times*, "and brokers and clerks swelled the throng that blackened Copley Square" in front of Trinity Church and filled the surrounding streets. Brooks's body had lain in state on the west porch of the church since 8:00 A.M. while fifteen thousand mourners filed by. "The eagerness of the outside multitude was so great" that the time for the funeral itself was delayed for an hour. Even then another three thousand viewers were unable to pay their respects. After the church service, prayers were offered in Copley Square and the crowd sang "Oh, God Our Help in Ages Past." "Meantime the great procession of 500 carriages had been forming." Thereafter the funeral cortege made its way across the Charles River to Cambridge and the Harvard Yard and thence to Mount Auburn Cemetery. The occasion, judged the *Times*, was "accompanied by evidences of public grief such as have not been manifested in this community for a generation," since the death of Abraham Lincoln.[2] The next day the *Boston Weekly Transcript* devoted the entire front page, including a two-column cut, to Brooks's life.

That the death of a preacher, much less that of an Episcopal bishop, should have elicited such a powerful public response is astonishing even for an age that drank deeply at the springs of oratory, religious or otherwise. Who was Phillips Brooks and what were the intellectual and personal abilities that he developed and that brought him adulation? Not that all had spoken well of him in his own time, nor would they in the following century. But clearly he was widely regarded in the Gilded Age. Those who disliked him expressed themselves with varying degrees of intensity.

On 7 April 1872 a precocious fourteen-year-old Unitarian, Alice Stone Blackwell, wondered in her diary why "Episcopalians make their ministers look so absurd by putting them into nightgowns with huge frills and flapping white wings."[3] A year later the teenager attended the annual festival at the Music Hall for the graduates of Boston's elite public schools. She was rather bored. The best part of the afternoon for Blackwell was the giving of bouquets to the girls. "Several people made speeches; Ralph Waldo Emerson was one, but we could not hear him," she wrote. "Also Phillips Brooks, who made a good speech but whom I consider an unctuous priest."[4] Since Brooks habitually dressed as other men and never wore a clerical collar or other priestly garb, it was a curious comment.

More serious were the allegations of Brooks's enemies in his own church. When in April 1891 he was elected bishop of Massachusetts, George F. Seymour, former dean of the General Theological Seminary in New York and then bishop of Springfield (Illinois), judged that as a result of the Bostonian's words and actions, "Satan has now insinuated himself into the very strongholds of Christianity, and sought to enter into a truce with its leaders and militant hosts."[5] It was strong language and from a powerful source. Brooks, it seems, had not only participated in an interdenominational service in a Congregational church on Good Friday and at the installation of Lyman Abbott as the successor to Henry Ward Beecher at the Plymouth Church, Brooklyn, but he had, according to Seymour, "*habitually*" permitted Unitarians "to receive the Holy Communion at his hands . . . [while] Rector of Trinity Church."[6]

Anglo-Catholics in the Episcopal church said they were shocked when Brooks made common cause with leaders of other denominations. But there was nothing new there: evangelical Episcopalians had been doing so for the better part of the nineteenth century.[7] What was irritating was the fame of the man, his outspokenness, and the conspicuousness of his actions. Brooks declared openly that he did not believe "the three-fold organization of the Christian ministry [bishops, priests, and deacons] or the existence of the episcopate is essential to the being of a Christian church." About as far as he would go in favor of his own denomination's polity was to suggest that something like the episcopate might emerge in the future in "the new Christian life, as it came forth in the development of the Church of the Apostles' time."[8]

For Brooks "Catholicity" clearly did not rest on loyalty to the historic precedent of bishops in succession so much as on future expectation of emerging Christian harmony. If he took seriously the Johannine injunction to oneness,[9] his optimism about its effect, not to mention its acceptance, seems visionary. Moreover, the Anglo-Catholics had a point: if one were to have an *Episcopal* church, one had better take seriously the claims its polity—and its very name—conveyed. For George Seymour and his allies, Catholicity had been controverted by papal claims to infallibility. "Rome by her present schemes of Church government repudiates catholicity," Seymour declared, "and brings back the local and narrow polity of Judaism."[10] Equally distressing to this leader of the movement to halt Brooks's consecration was the attitude of "charity, liberality [and] comprehensiveness" toward other Christian bodies.[11] As not a few historians have pointed out, there was nothing in the U.S. Constitution or in the American religious community that prohibited intolerance so long as none sought to suppress the rights of others.[12] Truth, Seymour was sure, "is always exclusive." Moreover, the "authoritative teaching of our Church, of the Church universal throughout all ages," has been that the sacraments "depend ultimately upon the Episcopate for their validity."[13] It was bad enough for Brooks to consort with Unitarians and Congregationalists, Seymour protested, but when "this Presbyter is a Bishop-elect, and is in prospect of being invested with the Episcopal office, and has made no retraction or explanation of such conduct . . . it becomes me to guard the trust of which I was put in charge."[14]

For Seymour, Brooks was hated and feared because his ideas and actions simply added to the confusion of modern life; for Seymour and for others, submission to ecclesiastical authority was an attractive alternative to a weightless tolerance.[15] Brooks seemed to threaten the "whole structure of the Liturgy, the rubrics, and the canons, and above all the recitation of the creed," the bishop of Springfield argued.[16] How could people say that they believed in Jesus Christ and then contradict the rules of the very church Christ had ordained, especially when such people were—as Seymour charged Brooks with being—Arians, Pelagians, "Quakers as regards the sacraments, that they are practically useless [and] Congregationalist as to the ministry"?[17]

For two months—May and June 1891—Brooks's opponents tried to derail the process of national approval that was required after each diocesan election.[18] During this time the several standing committees of the denomination's fifty-two dioceses were voting—agonizingly slowly for Massachusetts Episcopalians. Meanwhile the secular press carried almost daily accounts of the balloting. Some indication of the alarm that the bishop-elect caused in the church as a whole is seen in the fact that, in the end, 30 percent of the dioceses voted against him.[19] Finally, on 14 October 1891, Brooks was consecrated bishop in Trinity Church in the presence of the governor of the commonwealth, the mayor of Boston, the president of Harvard University, four hundred clergy, and seventeen hundred well-wishers.

His admirers rallied around, not only in numbers, but also in their rhapsodic affirmations of his character and goodness—so much so that the historian instinctively stands back unsure of the line between critical interpretation and hagiography, between analysis and protestation, and that perceptible area where the two coalesced in the minds of Brooks's contemporaries. Still, there is no doubt of his impact. With something of an air-drawn pen, Horace E. Scudder, future editor of the *Atlantic Monthly,* observed Brooks during an afternoon sermon when the "solitary pulpit light became the sole illumination of the church." Scudder noted the "glow of color upon the speaker's enkindled visage. All the church was dark. I could see a head here and there in the murkiness, but that intense light glowed more and more intensely. The darkness deepened the stillness, and the voice of the preacher, growing more fervid and passionate, came full and strong from that central glory in the gloom." The whole scene, wrote Scudder, "was the apotheosis of the pulpit."[20]

In the view of Alexander V. G. Allen, the church historian at the Episcopal Theological School in Cambridge, Brooks did not indulge in melodrama. On the contrary, he made demands on the minds of his auditors. Hearing him "was no luxury," judged Allen, "but it strained the tension of the hearer beyond any other experience of the art of oratory." Brooks was "free from guile and affectation," with a simple style, clear, rapid, precise, seemingly preaching "from deep personal, experience" and "utterly devoid of those pulpit mannerisms and affectations of which the world is weary." Moreover, Allen saw Brooks as neither "a moral, a social, nor a religious reformer" but one "who gave himself to his parish, and exclusively to the preacher's task and . . . was supremely interested in the building of the new Trinity Church." With the sick or with the depressed Brooks wisely abandoned the exhorter's role entirely. His muteness, however, appears to have been total, and at such pastoral times, Allen declares, "he sat down in silence by the bedside and no need was felt for words."[21] Given his piercing black eyes and imposing stature, no doubt for some the silence was intimidating rather than comforting.

To the homiletic and pastoral elements others added a prophetic strain. For William Lawrence, Brooks's successor as bishop of Massachusetts, he "was one of the prophets of his time [who] spoke for God" and seemed to have the prophet's assurance. During the "apparent victories of doubt and scepticism" in the late nineteenth century, Lawrence suggested, Brooks's confidence "kept him serene."[22] Charles W. Eliot was similarly impressed with the young minister's "prophetic" quality. When on 21 July 1865 Brooks was invited to give the invocation at Harvard's Commemoration Day for the school's Civil War dead, his electrifying prayer caused the future president of Harvard to believe that "a young prophet" had "arisen in Israel." Thirty years later Colonel Henry Lee, who had been chief marshal for the occasion, recalled Brooks and wrote: "From that moment the name of that inspired young man, till then unknown, became a household word." Similarly, William Reed Huntington, future rector of Grace Church in New York City, declared that "there went forth from his lips a fiery stream of thanksgiving and supplication the like of which I never knew."[23] What is clear is that Brooks, in a few moments, consciously or unconsciously upstaged the lions of the program: Ralph Waldo Emerson, James Russell Lowell, and Julia Ward Howe. Exactly what Eliot and Lawrence meant by the term "prophet," however, remains unclear.[24] "Power," perhaps; or as Brooks's cousin Henry Adams judged, "force." Adams placed Brooks at the head of a list that included Bret Harte, Henry James, H. H. Richardson, and John LaFarge—all of whom ranked in Adams's estimation as fathers of a school that "counted as force even in the mental inertia of sixty or eighty million people."[25]

More recent judgments, while not reflecting the lively opinions of Alice Stone Blackwell or George Seymour, have been generally critical, particularly in the second half of the twentieth century. In his landmark study *The Protestant Churches and Industrial America,* Henry F. May gives a carefully nuanced assessment of Brooks's conservative social outlook. A champion of African-American rights in Philadelphia during the Civil War, Brooks had, according to May, every reason to go on rebuking social sins, for "Boston was used to reforming ministers." Instead, he chose to emphasize "personal religion." May offers four points for the reader's consideration. First, Brooks was, like aristocrats of all ages, a believer that wealth, education, and social position were gifts of God "and that their accompanying responsibilities must not be ignored, either through modesty or cowardice." Second, Brooks claimed that poverty, while no positive blessing, bred certain virtues, "a closeness to reality, a mutual dependence, [and] the development of deeper faith." Third, Brooks was socially blind, for he "did not believe that great need was widespread in America during his lifetime." Fourth—and this is what separated the bishop from many of his prominent friends—Brooks "did not oppose social change with the panic, the stubborn reiteration, the violent denunciation of his contemporaries."[26]

With less subtlety, other historians have picked up on one side of May's conclusions. According to Winthrop Hudson, Martin E. Marty, and Sydney E. Ahlstrom, Brooks simply folded Christian faith into American culture and thus failed to criticize the devastation to the poor caused by the Industrial Revolution. Hudson states that Brooks, along with other Protestant preachers, embraced the gospel of wealth and by "investing the culture with intrinsic redemptive power, [left] . . . scant room for any special redemptive work of Christ."[27] Marty argues that Brooks was a "celebrity cleric" who underestimated the number and plight of America's poor and suggested that the "rich could be charitable and the poor could do much more to lift themselves by their bootstraps if they only followed the gospel which taught that wealth was a sign of divine favor."[28] Ahlstrom sees Brooks as an optimistic nationalist whose views kept him "untroubled by the inequities of American life."[29]

To others Brooks seems even more assuasive, this time theologically. T. J. Jackson Lears judges that he "blunted all the sharp edges in Protestant tradition and produced a bland religion of reassurance."

The omnipotence of God, unanticipated conversions, miracles as violations of natural law, and "cataclysmic interventions by an arbitrary Monarch" gave way to unfolding natural law, to humanism, and to the miraculous character of every common event.[30] At least one other historian picked up on Lears's view. Donald Fleming refers to Brooks as the "bland popular preacher" who, when chapel was made voluntary at Harvard in 1886, "drew from this the oddly Kierkegaardian but also Eliotian comfort [referring to Harvard's president] that if even fifty young men turned up voluntarily to say their prayers every morning, it would be 'the largest daily Protestant congregation in the world.'" Fleming argues that Brooks, in his support of Eliot's elective system, was little more than a prominent voice in the "final consummation of Protestantism . . . in the most Protestant of universities," a voice that declared that "God had become an elective at Harvard." And, he sarcastically adds, "Where else? Why not?"[31]

Something of the even-handedness of May is found in William B. Lawrence's article "The History of Preaching in America." Brooks "delivered thoughtful, scholarly sermons," writes Lawrence, but he was held "in a strange captivity" to the culture of his time. "Imbued with the optimism of the nation's growing prosperity [he was] . . . captivated by the spirit of the age. [Yet] for all his pastoral sensitivity and articulate handling of biblical texts, Brooks lacked a deep appreciation for what was happening in the society in the late nineteenth century . . . [to] the urban poor, who suffered from low wages, inadequate housing, and very little if any health care."[32]

The criticism nothwithstanding, in the hundred years since his death Brooks has had many admirers, and they come from both sides of the aisle in American Protestantism. In 1961, the liberal church historian Raymond W. Albright produced an appreciative biography that took into account new material on Brooks, though it made no attempt to place him in the context of his time.[33] From the conservative Christian phalanx on the other side have come supporters of Brooks such as Reuben Archer Torrey, one of the editors of *The Fundamentals,* and Warren W. Wiersbe, who in 1989 reissued Brooks's 1877 Lyman Beecher Lectures.[34] While Wiersbe finds Brooks often lacked an "orthodox" (i.e., substitutionary) doctrine of the atonement, in his view Brooks had "the heart of an evangelist, even though he might not have [had] the mind of a systematic theologian. The controlling force behind all of his ministry was the salvation of sinners."[35]

• • •

This study does not attempt to respond to the criticisms of either admirers or dispraisers of Phillips Brooks. Its purpose is to place him in the context of his time and culture, particularly to try to understand his personal, theological development as a young man and to explain his remarkable power and consistency as a preacher—something that was evident by the time he was twenty-four. Anyone seeking such a perspective on Brooks must be grateful for the contribution of Allen's two-volume biography, *The Life and Letters of Phillips Brooks*. Immediately after Brooks's death, while his memory was still fresh, Allen began an arduous decade of collecting and writing his subject's life-and-times. The nearly sixteen hundred pages of uncritical, facts-shoveled-on-facts constitute a valuable, if daunting, chronicle—though the "completeness" of Allen's work no doubt discouraged other would-be assessors. For nearly a century Trinity Church's famed rector has become an increasingly shadowy figure, at best relegated to the leadership of the liberal, or "broad church," movement within his own denomination, at worst merely a name and face on annual appointment calendars.

At the entrance to the library at the Episcopal Theological Seminary in Virginia, where Phillips Brooks studied in the late 1850s, there is a life-size, very heavy marble bust of that theological school's most famous graduate. In April 1965, in a waggish moment, some students who had been enjoying the spring evening managed with great effort to convey the bust, together with its pedestal, across the campus, into the chapel, and up into the pulpit, where they clothed the hollow-eyed, ghostly figure in a white surplice and black stole. Since this was perhaps the last lighthearted time before the student "revolution" in American education and the subsequent onset of "spirituality" in the church, the effect on the community at the service the next morning was hilarious.

My goal here is to make that sepulchral figure come to life, to turn the marble into flesh. It will not be done in the spirit of an exposé, or of one-upmanship, or of reduction to a blip on a psychological curve—though there will be psychological probing—or of a bloodletting that leaves its subject's life "dry of its vitality and authority."[36] Rather, by being carefully selective, in this monograph I examine Brooks's theological and intellectual lineage and context: his early, collegiate, and graduate education; his prejudices; the books and teachers he followed and, equally important, at times did not follow, as well as those he rejected outright; and, above all, his penetrating inquiry into the Gospels in his largely literary search for the distinctive features and substance of the person of Jesus of Nazareth. It is evident that simultaneously two strands of tradition influenced Brooks and nurtured his thinking: New England (Puritan/Reformed) theology and nineteenth-century Romanticism, which, taken together, are arguably the two principal sources of American Victorian culture.

Behind the corpus of Brooks's writings, his sermons and addresses, lay an eager mind and a critical spirit. Brooks read widely and constantly in the literature of antiquity and in that of his own time. But there was a center to that effort and a purpose—namely, to make the Christian proclamation "alive" to a generation that was well on the way to slipping its religious moorings. Thus another and perhaps less easily accomplished purpose of this study is to illuminate a life that touched and even exalted many lives with some grace. Here judgment is difficult. "Moral auditing" in biography, declares Marc Pachter, involves "balancing the legitimate rights of history against those of the individual."[37] But moral auditing also involves the right and obligation of the biographer not to put a marble bust on a pedestal, clothe it in religious vestments (even if only a black gown), and leave it in the pulpit. So far biographers and other commentators on Phillips Brooks, pro and con, have done little else.

This study also aims to make a contribution to our understanding of the decade immediately preceding the outbreak of the revolutionary struggle that we call the Civil War and that constituted the greatest crisis to date in the history of the American republic. If the intellectual, spiritual, and, in part, psychological development of a privileged and gifted young man can illuminate the culture of that age, theological and otherwise, so much the better.

Finally, there is the faith perspective. William Stringfellow, reflecting on history through the eyes of the New Testament, attests to a theological treatment of biography that has its own rules, its own way of writing, its own normative style and intention: the Word of God, incarnate first in Jesus of Nazareth and then in common history.[38] The primacy of the Word is often reduced to some other historical reality by secular historians and abstracted by theologians so as to render it "diminished, dismissed, omitted, or ignored." Stringfellow declares:

"I believe biography (and history), *any* biography and *every* biography, is inherently theological in the sense that it contains already—literally by virtue of the Incarnation—the news of the Gospel whether anyone discerns that. *We* are each one of us parables."[39] No doubt some more transparently than others.

1

New England Religion and Doting Parents

Phillips Brooks's roots were fixed in the soil of New England. He was fed by the character, the traditions, and the controversies of the place, especially those of the early nineteenth century. In colonial times, despite changes in the political and intellectual landscape, such as the twin arrivals of royal governors and Enlightenment modes of thought, New England presented a face of remarkable continuity and stability. All this changed with the successful completion of the revolution against Great Britain. "Like the first generation Puritans," remarks Harry Stout, "the patriots of 1776 were a new generation of 'founders'." Liberty, they and their successors discovered, cut two ways. Their battle cry of freedom had worked against the external enemy; when "it was lifted as easily against habits and traditions *within* American society . . . there was no telling how far Americans might go in reforming and restructuring" their institutions, or where it would all end.[1] Among other things, debilitating partisanship and unprecedented social rivalries led to the fear of decline among those with a proneness to write history, or those who were thereby induced to do so.[2] Among humbler—and less somber—folk, writes Nathan Hatch, "the pursuit of religious liberty became a root and branch assault upon the established order."[3] Not merely confined to the frontier or to the uneducated, this assault became a habit of mind well into the nineteenth century and in surprising places.

Brooks's parents reached young adulthood in the 1830s when the pursuit of religious liberty in New England reached its height. Not only were the revivalist successors of Jonathan Edwards continuing to challenge Old Light Calvinists, but Unitarians were rejecting both even as the revival wing of Unitarianism—the Transcendentalists—mocked well-fed but spiritually "corpse-cold" Bostonians. Meanwhile, in New Haven, Nathaniel William Taylor undermined the Calvinist doctrine of human depravity by divorcing sinfulness from human nature.

Among Episcopalians, old-fashioned high churchmen like Calvin Colton hated those "novelties," "histrionic exhibitions," and the "*histrionic* art" introduced by reforming avatars of the Oxford Movement.[4] Episcopalian mediators such as William A. Muhlenberg introduced a plan in 1853 for greater church unity within the American Anglican fold and beyond. Muhlenberg wanted liturgical flexibility and less-restrictive ordination requirements that would include adding the Episcopal imprimatur to willing clergy in other denominations. Accepted by the Episcopal Evangelicals and resisted by the high churchmen, it was talked to death. To Baptists and Presbyterians the memorial seemed bumptious.[5] In other denominations mediators such as Horace Bushnell sought to build bridges between Unitarians and Calvinists and ended up being cordially hated by both sides.

The result of this confusion, in the case of William and Mary Ann Phillips Brooks, was a search for authority, for stability, for a church that would reflect their level of education. They wished to be nurtured with rewarding forms of experience of the sacred, with feeling, as William had it, and not with rational lectures. Most important, their church must feed the intimate domestic Christianity that they, as Victorians, had come to prize.[6] Far from proving uninterested in doctrinal matters, however, as has been assumed by historians of this period with regard to the upper class, Mary wanted "correct" theology and in the reformed tradition at that.[7] Victorian piety, at least in this case, did not lead to mental dullness.

Phillips's mother was a determined woman. Diligently and purposefully she entered into three areas of life that were open to women in nineteenth-century America: religious vision, domestic discipline, and parenthood. In her watchfulness over her family, she appears to have been wholly preoccupied with them, if not reclusive. Since she came from the Massachusetts aristocracy, further social position held no allure—not that she felt awkward in the company of her contemporaries; indeed, she took advantage of the best that Boston afforded. Only twelve when her father, John Phillips of Andover, died in 1820 at the age of forty-five, and the fifth child of a large and now straitened family, she became a frequent visitor at the home of her maternal aunt, Nancy Gorham Brooks, the wife of New England's richest man, Peter Chardon Brooks. Nancy bore her husband thirteen children, and one more young person as an extra hand or companion did not create any difficulties. Uncle Peter made four million dollars in marine insurance and kept turning his money over in loans and mortgages (for which he never took over 6 percent interest, if we can believe his biographers). He seldom speculated in manufactures, railroads, or western lands, hated lotteries, believed in cold baths, and abstained from hard liquor. In Boston this was a prescription for success—except, perhaps, for the cold baths.[8]

Though assiduous in business, Peter was capable of detaching himself from everyday affairs to pursue cultural and religious interests. As Richard Hofstadter remarks of the family, the "ideal of civilized accomplishment never ceased to glimmer in their minds."[9] As much as any of the leading Bostonians, the Brookses exemplified the overlapping of the moral, literary, and cultural leaders—"the American gentry"[10]—with the emerging capitalist class. They and others wanted to humanize the industrial order and, as Daniel Walker Howe states, to "preserve certain patrician values while democratizing their application."[11] In terms of religion, they believed Unitarianism was the best, if not the only, vehicle for such preservation. At a crucial point in her life, Mary became a part of this larger, stimulating society. Under the solicitous eye of her uncle, important alliances were forged for her female cousins in particular. One daughter, Charlotte, married Edward Everett, future congressman and senator, governor of Massachusetts, minister to Great Britain, president of Harvard College, and opponent of General Andrew Jackson's policy of removal of the Cherokee nation. Another daughter, Abigail, married Charles Francis Adams, which "put the Adams family for the first time in eight generations on a firm financial footing."[12] A third daughter, Ann, married Nathaniel Frothingham, minister of the First Church. All of them, two clergy (Everett and Frothingham) and one layman (Adams), were Unitarians. Mary was too—almost, but with reservations. With the Brookses she went to Frothingham's First Church. She did not like it. In time she quit that fold, but not before she met and married young William Gray Brooks, her uncle Peter's nephew.

Mary's religious background was a curious patchwork shaped by the tradition of the Phillips family. That tradition was at first orthodox, Old Light Calvinist, not even Hopkinsian,[13] and had been for seven generations. Her paternal grandfather, Judge Samuel Phillips, built an extensive theological library in Andover, manufactured gun powder with which to fight the British, served Harvard for twenty years as an overseer, and judged his fellow citizens from the bench of the Essex Court of Common Pleas. Judge Phillips married the tall, beautiful Phoebe Foxcroft of Cambridge, who, without weakening the judge's doctrinal seriousness, brought a measure of wit and vivacity to the Phillips household. The judge wished to ensure that a "strictly orthodox variety of Calvinism" would be maintained in the education of the young, and in 1778, with the financial help of his father, Samuel, and his wealthy uncle John Phillips of Exeter, New Hampshire, founded Phillips Academy, Andover.[14] Two years after Samuel Phillips's death in 1802, Harvard bestowed the Hollis Chair of Divinity on the liberal Congregationalist Henry Ware, Sr. As a result, Andover turned against Cambridge, and in 1808 Mary's father, with the help of his mother, founded Andover Theological Seminary. Against the common Unitarian foe, Andover conservatives like Jedidiah Morse made peace with the followers of Jonathan Edwards, Samuel Hopkins, and Joseph Bellamy. As a result, New Divinity men, including Leonard Woods and Moses Stuart, assumed positions of lasting authority at the seminary. The Phillipses, for a while at least, preferred to keep their souls in Westminster purity and diligence unalloyed by compromises.[15]

Then, two things happened. First, sometime around 1810, the North Parish Church, adjacent to John and Lydia Phillips's home in North Andover, went Unitarian. Second, John became ill. He and his wife and daughters began to attend North Parish instead of traveling each Sabbath to the trinitarian church in Andover.[16] There may have been social and family reasons as well for their action—or for their inertia. In any case, the Phillips daughters were registered in the North Parish Church—all except Mary.[17]

Did the Calvinism of her ancestors reappear by generation? Was she influenced by her grandmother, Phoebe Foxcroft; or by her own inquisitiveness about her family's heritage; or by her reading? We shall perhaps never know. It is certain that she was brought up as a Unitarian. It is equally certain that she underwent a change back to the Calvinism of her grandparents, which she found replicated in the Evangelical party in the Episcopal church. It is some measure of the extent of the change in her mind that she distrusted the theology of Horace Bushnell. As late as 1864, she wrote to her son Phillips, then the Episcopal rector of Holy Trinity Church, Philadelphia, of her strong distaste for Bushnell's sermons: "I am so shocked by them that I cannot refrain from warning you against them as being a preacher of the Cross of Christ." The sermons were "nothing better than [the] Unitarianism that I suffered under all my life." They "tear the view of Christ's vicarious suffering all to pieces."[18] Her final word on Bushnell's attempt to show that the Unitarian emphasis on Jesus as moral teacher and exemplar was consistent with orthodoxy was unmistakably negative.[19] Still, there was a touch of conspiratorial humor, when she wrote: "No, my dear child; remember, you have promised to preach Christ and *Him crucified* in the *true* meaning of the words, and I charge you to stand firm. If you do read the book, I would love to see you come out with a scorching criticism of it."[20] Her son had indeed read *The Vicarious Sacrifice* (1866), and liked it, so no such review came forth. In 1877, in his famous Yale lectures on preaching, Phillips even advised his audience to "turn to Barrow, Tillotson, or Bushnell" for broad treatment of great biblical themes.[21]

Whatever early convictions Mary had while living in Boston with the Brookses, she kept to herself. Genteel poverty suggested prudence. Love played its part as well. Her future husband, William, had come from Portland, Maine, at the age of nineteen to enter the dry-goods business in Boston. The two were married in 1833. William too was a Unitarian; in fact, he shortly became a member of the standing committee of the First Church, where the couple worshiped regularly for six years.[22] When Nathaniel Frothingham—the "artful dodger of the Unitarians," as Emerson called him[23]—finally used the term "Unitarian" in a Sunday sermon in 1835, Mary would have none of it. (She had unaccountably missed the Thursday Lectures where her cousin had been using the term ever since 1824.[24]) When Nathaniel employed it on the Sabbath, however, the fat was in the fire. Yet she must have known from her youth in the North Parish Church what the issues were and the names that went with them. We may only conclude that by the mid-1830s the line was so drawn that Mary felt it necessary to decide once and for all, which she did—for orthodoxy.

There was another element in the crisis of religion in William and Mary's household. It came to a head, perhaps not accidentally, in 1838 when Emerson delivered his vivid and sonorous Divinity School Address at Harvard, a speech whose color in that "refulgent summer" lit up the drabness and complacency of Boston's liberal religion.[25] The Enlightenment had received its most telling romantic challenge, and that challenge had come now from Concord as well as from Andover.

A few months later, William confided in his diary, prosaically enough: "Wife was never much pleased with Mr. F's style of preaching, and after a good deal of consideration & reflection, we concluded to change and have got a pew at St. Paul's (Episcopalian) where Rev Dr Stone officiates." He found it "unpleasant changing our habits & places of resort," for he felt attached, as he said, to "the Unitarian Church having been brought up to that doctrine." Still, he could not say that he had "so much horror & repugnance to the orthodox sect as many have."[26]

According to William, Frothingham's sermons were "very beautiful, always distinguished for fine writing"; but, perhaps reflecting Mary's reaction, he added: "they left nothing behind them, they are too sentimental, too mystical, not practical enough & like Unitarian preaching too cold, nothing to take hold of and interest the feelings."[27] Not until 30 May 1847, nearly a decade later, would William become confirmed in the Episcopal church, which for him was a solemn occasion. To record "my thoughts of this day would be an utter impossibility," but he vowed "to always keep the actions and feelings of this day in view, never to lose sight of the principles which activated me to go forward as I did this day and join in the rite of confirmation." He wished nothing so much as that thereafter he and his wife "may walk together as one in Christ, as our head and guide."[28] Mary had done her work well. But it is noteworthy that the two strands, the Calvinist and the Unitarian, lay in the background of Phillips's life, for his career, like that of his mentor, Horace Bushnell, was in part dedicated to bridging the chasm between them. He did so by discovering an ideal beyond them both.

What attracted Mary and eventually William to the Episcopal church? It was not at first the liturgy. On 1 November 1840, William wrote: "it is now about a year since we began to attend the Episcopal church—it was quite a change to make both in the manner of the service & also in the matter and sentiments that are preached." He found the rector too argumentative, the morning service too long and tedious, but the afternoon one—presumably nonliturgical—"very agreeable," adding that they did not wish to "go back to the dull & dry services of the Unitarian church we left." Seven years and one rector later, William found the Christmas liturgy "comforting & elevating accompanied by the Communion."[29]

The Brookses could have gone back to a trinitarian Congregational church. There was always the Hanover Street Church, where Lyman Beecher had been and gone by 1832, though that Edwardsian Calvinist had left a certain taint. Beecher's country accent and homely, unsophisticated ways had not endeared him to genteel Bostonians. In addition, his high visibility had tarred his church with the brush of Charles Grandison Finney or Nathaniel W. Taylor of Yale—or of both. Did revivalist shenanigans awake tribal memories and given credence to the constant Anglican drumbeat about the evils of un-Anglican worship, with its "wholesale reliance upon extemporaneous productions of the mind . . . the 'vanity and vapours of an empty skull'"?[30] Not likely, since Episcopalians had changed and colonial taunts were a thing of the past.[31] Small numbers and a vast field of missionary opportunity had wonderfully transformed them. Now more modest, they even added a certain revivalist freedom to the "decent appointed worship of the Church"[32]—but just enough, not too much. While Episcopalian Evangelicals had much in common with revivalists, there were social safeguards that assured a measure of decorum. No doubt for many, Mary Brooks's decision would support the belief that "in the American mind generally is an inherent capacity for Anglican-like response to regular, orderly custom."[33] Possibly. But regular, orderly custom wears a number of noble faces. That some were more eminent and aquiline than others is certain.

For the Brookses, then, there was an additional dimension: the Episcopal church's two leading parishes (out of three), Trinity and St. Paul's, were socially acceptable. Their people were from the educated class. Both were also theologically evangelical,[34] and the Evangelicals were in the ascendancy in the denomination. Episcopal Evangelicals were also doctrinally strict and, with the exception of double predestination, held all other points of Calvinism,[35] including intellectual assent to God's perfection, humankind's fall from original righteousness, total depravity,[36] the absolute need for salvation, the atonement and mediation of Jesus Christ, sanctification by divine grace, and the call to live according to the Gospel.[37] It was all very bracing. There was also a check on excessive emotionalism and fanaticism. Ecumenically minded leadership from Bishop Alexander Griswold of New England (except Connecticut) led to good relations with other evangelical Christians, and that made the change easier yet for those hankering after Old Light Calvinism. But the most significant drawing card for Mary Brooks may well have been simply that John S. Stone, who lead the parish, was a graduate of Andover Theological Seminary.

Mary entered wholeheartedly into the life of St. Paul's. So, increasingly, did her husband. In fact, their home became an extension of their church to a marked degree. Mary's religious vision eventually led her to the fervent wish that as many as possible of her six children—all boys[38]—should enter the ministry. It was a desire in which she was eventually joined by her husband, and they were not disappointed: Phillips, Frederick, Arthur, and John Cotton became Episcopal clergymen.

Phillips was brought up in a household that exemplified Victorian domestic discipline with, as Anne Rose remarks, "its commitment to self-control, social order, and absolute values."[39] James McPherson observes that "affection and encouragement of self-discipline replaced repression and corporal punishment as the preferred means of socialization in middle-class families."[40] There were family prayers every evening; Bible stories were told to the children at bedtime; the rule on Sundays was church in both the morning and the afternoon; each week the boys memorized a hymn, which was recited on Sunday evening—nothing new in any of this, for theirs was the pattern of many Victorian homes. Except that Mary instilled her special seriousness and fervor into these occasions. Some measure of her success is evident in the fact that by the time he went to college, Phillips knew by heart some two hundred hymns.[41] For her family prayers and teaching, Mary provisioned herself at Dr. Stone's Bible class, where "he explained Christian doctrines, or commented on the Epistle and Gospel for the day, or at times took up the books of Scripture."[42] The figures in them she made heroic for her sons.

In all other respects the Brooks home seems to have had a minimum of rules, a certain freedom, and a good deal of noisy exuberance. There was plenty of skating, sledding, hiking, and the like, though little or no organized sports.[43] The boys learned an ordered way of life, but nowhere "did there seem to be any resemblance to rigidity of discipline."[44] Nonetheless, there was a constant parental patrol respecting the boys. Something of this can be seen in William's warning on smoking when Phillips was in his final year of graduate school. "I was surprised to find your letter of last evening strongly 'perfumed' with tobacco," wrote the elder Brooks. "I have tried to think I was mistaken but I cannot be & must beg you again, if you value my good opinion or my wishes, you will at once practice total abstinence in this matter." Phillips's mother even wanted to know how he arranged his clothes![45]

As a parent, Mary Brooks lavished affection on her sons—doted on them, in fact—and when they were not at home she constantly made up packages of gifts to send to them. She also continued to hand out advice freely. When in old age his mother moved back to Andover, Phillips, then the busy rector of Trinity Church, took the train to dutifully call on her once a week. "Philly" was named after Mary's family, and he seems to have been her favorite. When in the spring of his final year at theological school in Virginia he decided to take the rectorship of the Church of the Advent in Philadelphia, he received a congratulatory letter from his mother. It was, she believed, an "uncommon opening[.] . . . you seem to have weighed it [the decision] so faithfully and deliberately and prayerfully. . . . I feel perfectly sure now that it is the place for you and that God has *called* you to it." She added: "I long to fly to you—I long to talk with you."[46] She even wanted to pick the text for his first sermon—though she did not.[47] When she read the manuscript, however, she liked it because, as Phillips's father wrote, it contained "so much Gospel."[48] Later, in 1859, when Phillips was ordained, Mary confided in her notebook: "How God has honored me and rejoiced my heart this day & answered all my prayers by calling my dear child into his vinyard." She prayed that her son would "be faithful & devoted to his master's work, until his life's end."[49] Phillips, who was forty-four when his mother died in 1880, wrote to a friend: "My mother has been the centre of all the happiness of my life."[50]

Still, Mary was no fool. She recognized that there comes a time "when it is not well to follow or question your boy too closely." Aware of the onset of adolescence and the changed relationship that occurs between mothers and sons at that time, she knew when not to make demands and almost clinically observed the inevitable distancing: "Suddenly these confidences [of childhood] cease; the affectionate son becomes reserved and silent, he seeks the intimate friend-ship of other lads, he goes out, he is averse to telling where he is going or how long he will be gone. He comes in and goes silently to his room. All this is a very startling change to the mother, but it is also her opportunity to practice wisdom by loving, and praying for, and absolutely trusting her son."[51]

The intensity of concern, evidenced by the number of letters the Brooks family wrote to each other when anyone was absent from the home, was one thing. The intellectual stimulation of their "back par-lor," where they all gathered to read, study, write themes, and, in the father's case, do accounts in the evening, was another—one that left a lasting impression. When Phillips was in theological school, his father wrote him: "William and George are deeply interested now in the study of Geometry, devoting three hours a day to it & varying it by Architecture."[52] Anne Rose might well be writing of the Brooks family circle when she judges that the "reliable routines of middle-class conventionality made possible a quest that rarely was socially disruptive, but often was radical in the expansive range of feeling and imagination cultivated."[53] Certainly this expansiveness was true of Phillips. In adulthood, feeling and imagination, and the ability to express them, blossomed in him.

Emotional maturity came slowly, however, and, as we shall see, without perhaps that greater freedom to order one's own ways that marks the passage to adulthood. The brothers habitually referred to themselves, even when grown men, as the "Brooks Boys." At least with Phillips, there was the sense that the domestic scene of his child-hood home could never be repeated, certainly not with the same "per-fection." As Raymond Albright astutely observes, "Phillips almost frantically tried to hold on to the security of the earlier days."[54] The back parlor was not so much stifling as daunting, a memory of a golden time that was at once inhibiting and inspiring. The family did not seem to be able to leave it alone, for there was simply nothing comparable. Unlike Henry David Thoreau, Phillips was, however, capable of taking some decisive steps toward personal freedom, as we shall see. Yet he never was able fully to break the strong ties to the family circle or, which is more likely, to replicate those ties himself in a family of his own.[55] For this limitation, if it was that, his mother was largely responsible. In a letter to Phillips the year he graduated from theological school, William wondered aloud whether any of his sons had any idea "of the extreme, incessant, and maternal anxiety she [their mother] constantly feels for each one of you." Such anxiety and love, he wrote, "ought to be repaid back a thousand-fold and then the debt would still remain."[56] Even given the Victorian penchant for expressing feelings in heightened form, it was a heavy burden to lay on a son.

Phillips seems also to have been the favorite of his father. Toward the end of 1855, William wrote comments in his diary about each of his children, three of whom were then in young adulthood or close to it. His namesake had attended but "part of the terms of [the] Latin & English high schools" and at the age of sixteen had been "an apprentice to the Dry Goods business [his own occupation] in the store of Nichols, Pierce Co. . . . [He] then went to Sweetzer, Godkin Co. where he still remains though past his majority." Recalling his son William's bout with typhus in 1845, the elder Brooks then spoke of his concerns: "His health has always been delicate and [I have] some fears that he may be of a consumptive habit."[57] But William Jr. fooled them by surviving four of his younger brothers and living on into the twentieth century.

When William turned to Phillips there was a marked change. His second son, he wrote, "had entered the Latin [Boston Latin School] with William but while William left & went to the English High, Phillips continued on and graduated a medal scholar in 1851." Then came four years at Harvard College, where Phillips "sustained well his part and graduate[d] handsomely & creditably in 1855." There also were no doubts in the father's mind about either accomplishments or health:

All his course through college was marked by diligence, attention & good behaviour; before he graduated he had applied for the situation of Usher in the City Latin School, and in August of this year among nine other applicants, he received the appointment and is now engaged in that responsible occupation which brings him a salary of 1000 dollars per annum. He has also always enjoyed good health and been remembered for his large growth and manly form; at the age of 16 he weigh[ed] 173 and was six feet 4 in[ches] in height.[58]

The elder Brooks should have been more cautious. Failure was already stealing along and about to overtake the favorite.

George, the third son, was also a "medal scholar" at the Boston Latin School but proved not to have an interest in the classics and "in 1855 entered the Lawrence Scientific School in the class of chemistry."[59] Though pleased with George's achievements, William withheld praise comparable to that bestowed on Phillips. At the time of writing, the other three boys were still young and in school.

Relations among the brothers appear to have been particularly close, often jocular. To George, the family's aspiring scientist and farmer, Phillips began a letter with one long, deliberately barbarous sentence:

> Do me the favor to take your geometry & shut it up with William in the closet room in the house & get him to put a chair against the door: then get your Muck-Manual & all the late numbers of the *New England Farmer* & put them under the heaviest copy of Leverett's *Lexicon* that you can find (then I guess *they're* safe) & put your feet up on the sofa, (if mother objects to this last arrangement just take her pet tidy to rest them on & keep your feet clean) & so be wholly at ease & in a state of perfect "receptivity," as the philosophers say to imbibe like the spongiest kind of a sponge the four pages of nothing that I am bound to give you before I get off this uncommonly lumpy cushion. (You don't object to long sentences do you?)[60]

· · ·

William's extensive diaries provide a wide window onto Boston politics, economics, and religious affairs over many decades of the nineteenth century. From his father Phillips acquired similar powers of observation. The elder Brooks's diaries reveal that he was a man who was careful for his business, trusted by family and associates, precise, accurate, orderly, a keen observer of the ways of the world. When Peter Chardon Brooks died in 1849, William was privy to the contents of the older man's will, and after listing the bequests, he wrote: "This comprehends the whole; there is not a public donation of any kind & but very little out of his immediate family, and none out of his family. . . . we were all much surprised to find anything to us." He added with obvious distaste, "as his public bequests are nothing, the community will soon forget him."[61]

Phillips reflected his father's influence at an early age in the care with which kept his possessions, with his penchant for detail and hard work,[62] even in the manual dexterity and penmanship that both shared.[63] They also shared a carefulness, even frugality, about money. William complained that the high cost of pew rents, in addition to the charities and contributions, "come heavy upon a man of moderate means and large family dependent upon him."[64] When Phillips asked his father for financial aid, he wrote back: "your request was very reasonable and I wish you would not feel so bad about asking when you want. . . . I think you have grown very economical, not that I think you were ever extravagant."[65]

A conservative man of broad sympathies, William Brooks tried to be fair, and sometimes succeeded. When Benjamin Fenwick, the aristocratic Roman Catholic bishop of Boston, died in 1846, the elder Brooks noted that he was "much beloved & as unobjectionable as one of that religion can be; he has exerted a good influence on the Irish & has always cooperated with the city authorities." He also noted the irony of Fenwick's death "on the anniversary of the burning of the convent at Charlestown . . . a disgraceful scene."[66] William thought well of Fenwick's successor, John Fitzpatrick, who "was educated in our public schools and is said to be a learned & excellent man."[67] Phillips was doubtless influenced as well by his father's benevolence toward other churches. When, in New England, Christmas began to be celebrated in the 1840s, the elder Brooks found it to be a means toward greater charity. On 25 December 1846, he noted that "St. Paul's Church was very crowded. . . . among the auditors I noticed a clergyman [each] of the Orthodox [Congregational], Baptist & Unitarian societies which shows that the bitterness of sectarianism is giving way." There was, he wrote, no better proof of this than "the increase of the observance of this holy day."[68] Phillips reflected his father's attitude when, in 1842, he referred to a fiery Baptist preacher who denounced other churches during a visit to Boston as "vulgar and indecent."[69]

Though free from anti-Irish nativism, William was less tolerant of abolitionists. At the same time, in 1857, that he feared the slave trade was "stealthily" beginning again in the South, he spoke angrily of the "rabid abolitionists"[70] and particularly of that "notorious abolitionist, Wendell Phillips," who was his wife's cousin.[71] He disliked Theodore Parker (whom his sons found exciting, if heretical), had little love for the British, and noted "how small stuff royalty is made of whether male or female."[72] When in 1853 Harriet Beecher Stowe was feted in England by rich and poor alike, William thought she was "being treated as foolishly as we Yankees have treated some English travelers." He added that *Uncle Tom's Cabin* only "pretends to be a true relation of slavery"[73]—though it is unlikely that he read the book. Phillips and his brothers would prove to be far more critical of slavery than their father.

William was politically a Whig. On 19 May 1860, with a degree of hauteur, he expressed his dislike for the Republican presidential nominee, Abraham Lincoln, and his running mate, Hannibal Hamlin of Maine, calling their nominations "very singular" and "done as the Democrats did when they nominated Frank Pierce, took candidates but little known. . . . One hundred guns was fired on the Common today in honor of the nomination, not the men." When, on election day, John A. Andrew, a Republican, was chosen governor of Massachusetts, William declared that "the state has suffered a disgrace." He was not a little annoyed by "my sons [who] have taken the popular side of republicanism and like young politicians generally have been rather sanguine and not at all times so courteous and considerate as they will be when they have seen more of politics and age." As a result, he wrote, "sadness and gloom" closed 1860.[74] However, a change in his view slowly began to take place. In March 1861, he breathed a sigh of relief that, despite threats from the South, Lincoln's inauguration had gone off well: "he is President & if his inaugural is any test, he will make a good one."[75] When both Andrew and Lincoln were overwhelmingly reelected, William judged it "a splendid result"[76]—and so on through the deeply felt tragedy of Lincoln's assassination. What is significant here is the man's curiosity, practicality, and integrity—and the independence of Phillips's views from his father's.

From the 1840s on, William's interest in religion had increased. He was a good deal more critical of his newfound church than his wife, and with the same discerning eye that marked his son Phillips,[77] he became a good judge of the clergy. When Alexander Vinton, the rector of St. Paul's Church, left in October 1858, the elder Brooks noted that "he has been our spiritual guide & advisor and through his means with God's blessing myself with William & Phillips have been brought into the Church." He found Vinton a "powerful and eloquent preacher and as such has stood . . . at the head of the Episcopal Church in the Diocese." But, he added, the man showed "naturally indolent habits, [and] his parochial duties have been neglected."

Worse, "he has that detestable and dirty habit of smoking and chewing tobacco to an alarming and extravagant excess." When William heard that the rector was going on to a larger sphere, he wondered if it was due to the fact that over the sixteen years in Boston he had gotten together a "good stock of sermons" so that "he would naturally have more leisure." Still, in his opinion Vinton was "a man of superior talents," even if he was inclined to make only "one ceremonious call upon a family in a year & . . . [then have] no other intercourse with them."[78]

William's involvement in religious matters—and, as a result, in his second son's career—was increased by the religious events of 1857–58, which he referred to as "a great revival . . . [to be] remembered as equal in interest to the great Whitefieldian revival." He and his wife attended prayer meetings, for which "there is no machinery at work but it seems really to be an outpouring of the Spirit. A large proportion of the meeting this morning were men, business men; four or five churches are opened every morning for prayer & inquiry meeting and the business men's meeting at the Old South Chapel at noon is daily crowded—it is the same in New York & Philadelphia, surely a remarkable time and such as we have never before seen."[79]

Phillips's parents were now more than ever united in pressing for what they wanted from him. For his part, young Brooks had confided in his diary in the previous year (1856) his struggle over a career and his anger at the sheer strength of his parents' influence. "If I am to choose a life for *myself,* which I am to live and for which I am to answer," he wrote, then "let the choice be—*really mine.*" He would listen to his advisers, "but no dictation." The twenty-year-old cried, "Without presumption or vanity, humbly earnestly, and firmly, I claim my own human and divine right to my own life."[80] A month later, just after Phillips had gone off to the theological school in Virginia, William complained that "being of a diffident, sensitive disposition he has refrained from coming out so openly as I could have wished and in fact to this time he [has] not communicated." He continued: "it is the first break we have had in our domestic circle and a favorite one among us all has left."[81] Phillips's mother wrote to him: "the little boys miss you as *teacher* and playfellow. We all miss you, Philly, for you was very kind and pleasant when you was at home."[82] A year later, Mary joined William in complaining about reticence: "Do write often, my dear son and express your feelings freely." He would gladden his parents hearts, she told him, if only he would open up more. To which she added: "If you knew how much and how often you are in our thoughts and prayers, you would feel a stronger bond of sympathy with home. Not that I think you are deficient in that feeling, but it would be stronger."[83]

Just as Mary knew when to grant adolescents their freedom, William had the sense to stay out of his son's affairs, even though at times he was critical. There was not a little grace in a letter to Phillips in early 1859, when William commented on the young man's professional future: the decision of where he would exercise his ministry "must be left very much to yourself to act . . . as you think best, being on the spot and having good advisers about you." Phillips's future, he declared, was one to be held in the highest respect, the "glorious work of a preacher."[84]

· · ·

The "first break in the domestic circle," which William earlier lamented, was to prove permanent. Except for visits, Phillips would not return to Boston to live until 1869, and then he would live alone. Toward Christmas 1865, he wrote a letter to his mother from Germany. It subtly reminded her that for some time he had been independent: "You cannot think how strange it seems to be writing in this little German inn, knowing that you will read it in the old back parlor at home, where you have read my letters from Cambridge, Alexandria, and Philadelphia."[85] But that domestic schoolroom his strong-willed parents had created was only partially put behind him. Though they had, during those winter evenings, done their work well, they were only a part of the texture of their son's life. The maturation and education of Phillips Brooks were a good deal more complex and more interesting.

2

Growing Up in Boston's High Culture

The city of Boston in which Phillips Brooks grew up was growing along with him—nearly doubling its population, from 84,400 in 1840 to 177,800 in 1860.[1] But Boston in the 1850s was not the metropolis of a century later, with its huge office buildings. Mid-nineteenth-century Boston was intimate; it seemed to be made for pedestrian sociability, if not for what we would today consider comfort. Buildings were undramatic, generally uniform in height, not too tall; signs over shops matched each other and did not clash with the building's architecture; awnings shielded customers in the summer, when heat and dust were problems; and the skyline was dominated by church spires that rose higher than the surrounding structures. Steeples of the Old South Meeting House, the Federal Street Church, the Park Street Church, and, by 1862, the Arlington Street Church pierced the sky. Later, after the Civil War, they were joined by the Church of the Covenant, the First Baptist Church, the New Old South Church, and the famed Trinity Church—all in the new Back Bay area. Old photographs show the city's "face," writes Robert Campbell: "windows suggest, as eyes do, intelligences behind them looking out; buildings have tops and bottoms like hats and boots. Lined up and jostling one another like seniors at their class portrait, they smile and frown across the street space."[2] Boston was social, alive, and reassuring, not frightening in speed and impersonality.

Sanitation was another matter, however. Wells and sewage facilities were in close proximity, and there was no municipal public water system until the end of the century. Typhus was a menace, as were other diseases related to overcrowding. Still, Boston had developed an extensive hospital system by mid-century: the Massachusetts General Hospital (1811–21), with its branch for mental disease, McLean Hospital (1816); the Massachusetts Charitable Eye and Ear Infirmary (1824); Perkins Institute for the Blind (1832); the Massachusetts School for Feeble Minded Children (1839); and the Massachusetts College of Pharmacy (1852).

High culture belonged to Boston unlike any other city in America, and that culture became increasingly cosmopolitan during the years when Brooks was growing up. In 1852 Boston's Music Hall, which seated two thousand, was completed; two years later the three-thousand-seat opera house, the Boston Theatre, opened its doors with Beethoven's *Fidelio*.[3] The Handel and Haydn Society (1815) was joined by the Harvard Musical Association (1837) and finally by the Boston Symphony Orchestra (1880).

Until the later decades of the century, Boston was also the literary heart of America, with five daily newspapers by 1850 and two of the nation's most exceptional literary journals in the *North American Review* (1815) and the *Atlantic Monthly* (1857). The Boston Public Library (1830), incorporated in 1848, was the first free municipal library in the world, the second largest in America (after the Library of Congress), and by the beginning of the next century had the largest free circulation of any library in the world (1,529,111 volumes in 1907). Its pre–Civil War special collections ran from Spanish and Portuguese works to nearly complete sets of British and American public documents; from mathematics, the history of women, and music to the anthropology and ethnology of Europe; plus a hundred thousand volumes on the history, biography, geography, and literature of the United States. Other notable institutions included the Athenaeum (1807); the famed Massachusetts Historical Society (1791), which was the oldest such organization in America; the New England Historic Genealogical Society (1845); the American Academy of Arts and Sciences (1780); and the Boston Society of Natural History (1830).

The measure of concern for knowledge through formal education can also be seen in the fact that between 1821 and 1848 fourteen new elementary schools were founded. In the years immediately after the Civil War, higher education rocketed in metropolitan Boston: Boston College (1860, Roman Catholic); the Massachusetts Institute of Technology (1865), the largest purely scientific and technical school in the nation for decades to come, which opened its doors to women as well as men; Boston University (1869, Methodist); the New England Conservatory of Music (1867), also coeducational; Massachusetts Normal Art School (1873); and the School of Drawing and Painting of the Museum of Fine Arts (1876).

As Douglass Shand-Tucci observes, the "city's overall ambition [was] to take its place among the 'chief capitals of the world.'"[4] To do this, Boston took as its model in the 1850s and 1860s the architectural splendor of Second Empire Paris and adorned itself with Frederick Law Olmstead's "emerald necklace" of parks (1875), stretching from the Boston Common (1634) and the Boston Public Garden (1859), down Commonwealth Avenue, with its four rows of trees, to the Back Bay Fens, to Olmstead Park and Jamaica Pond, with the Arnold Arboretum on one side and Franklin Park (527 acres) on the other. The whole comprised more than twenty-three hundred acres with a hundred miles of pathways for walks, drives, and rides.

Like most cities, however, not all parts of Boston were so inviting. Kenneth Stampp has observed that increasing lawlessness, homicides, the garroting of people on the streets for purposes of robbery, police corruption, counterfeiting, and armed burglaries plagued American cities in the 1850s.[5] Large areas of Boston were well on their way to becoming wastelands, especially the South End, which would be referred to as a "social wilderness" and "the city wilderness."[6] Not surprisingly, the Brooks boys were forbidden to play beyond the family property after dark.[7]

· · ·

At age eleven, Phillips Brooks was accepted at Boston's—and America's—oldest and most renowned school, the Boston Latin School. Founded in 1635, a year before Harvard College, Boston Latin maintained the highest educational standards, from which it has not budged.[8] From its inception the school was intellectually nonegalitarian. It imposed strict discipline and, well into the nineteenth century, corporal punishment on its students. At the same time, since it was a free school, Boston Latin was socially democratic. Eventually it became blind not only to economic distinctions but, in the twentieth century, to racial and ethnic ones as well. Academic excellence alone admitted students, who, like the faculty, were increasingly Irish, Jewish, Italian, Armenian, African, and other non-Anglo-Saxon nationalities. Theodore White observes that the school "held absolutely anyone was free to enter. And the school was free to fail and expel absolutely anyone who did not meet its standards."[9]

As a result of Boston Latin's policies, after the Civil War the elite, Anglo-Saxon Protestants began sending their sons to expensive, segregated boarding schools. But it was also the urbanization of America itself, and the increasing presence of the very poor in those cities, that made the rich move their children's education to the secluded countryside. In 1884, in the "Preface to Records," the trustees of Groton School specifically declared that "owing to . . . the rapid growth of large cities, there was a demand for such an institution."[10] Boston Latin had no choice but to stay in its place.

From the very beginning this remarkable school sought to equip those who were able to sustain its mental and behavioral discipline with the tools for writing, rational discourse, and debate—endeavors that were to be undertaken with a minimum of verbiage. White sums it up best: "The Latin School taught the mechanics of learning with little pretense of culture, enrichment, or enlargement of horizons."[11] In doing so, it contributed immeasurably to Boston, to Massachusetts, and to the nation. Its roster of graduates boasts more illustrious leaders than any other school in America: Cotton Mather, Benjamin Franklin, John Hancock, Ralph Waldo Emerson, Wendell Phillips, Charles W. Eliot, George Santayana, Bernard Berenson, and Leonard Bernstein, to name but a few. Not the least of these by any means was Phillips Brooks.[12]

Brooks's attendance at the Boston Latin School, from 1846 to 1852, marked the last years of a curriculum that had been essentially unchanged since the seventeenth century. The course of study was dominated by Latin, Greek, English composition, declamation, geography, and Greek and Roman history. In fact, the only subject outside this regular fare was a single drawing class, instituted in 1843.[13] By and large the curriculum fostered an exhortatory forensic style of leadership, one that sought heroes and an ideal.[14] Conspicuously absent was the study of modern languages, English and American literature, science, medieval and modern history, and athletics of any kind.[15]

As a schoolboy, Brooks learned Latin and Greek with apparent ease. He also absorbed and retained details of Greek and Roman history, which, since the Renaissance, Western culture as a whole had thought more worthwhile than biblical, medieval, or modern studies. When he was in theological school, writing a paper on the atonement, he naturally drew examples of expiatory sacrifice from Homer and Hesiod, from passages of Caesar's showing Gallic sacrificial practices, from the battle deaths of the Decii, and from Phoenician and Carthaginian worship.[16]

Along with history, English composition proved to be equally important to Brooks. Themes were written on a regular basis on subjects no doubt assigned by the teacher. At first his grades were not always high. The best mark one could receive for a composition at the Latin School was 20, and Brooks's grades varied considerably: "California" (10), "Slavery" (15), "The Evils of War" (10), "The Government of Thoughts" (12), "The Pleasures of Memory" (18), "Solitude" (19), "Selfishness" (18), "Books" (19), and "Independence" (19). His essays were literate but not outstanding, though his writing improved as time went on. "Solitude," a somewhat stilted essay, is typical of an adolescent who wonders what it is like to *feel* alone but has never really *been* alone for any length of time. "How delightful it is to flee from its [life's] busy scenes," he warbled, "and to seek repose in solitude; to feel that no human eye can see, and no human voice intrude to mar the quiet and the peace with which the soul is surrounded."[17] Less artful—and more revealing—was his description nine years later of a boyhood Thanksgiving Day at the Brooks household: "First to church. Then a tremendous dinner. Then a quarrel for the best sofas [in the back parlor], then about the middle of the afternoon a general waking up & continuous uproar from then till bed-time."[18] Solitude in the Brooks household was rare.

As he grew into adolescence, Brooks was a hard person to get to know—thanks to his "Massachusetts frostiness," as one friend put it. But reticence had its reward in the eyes of another, who declared that Brooks seemed not to be "perpetually prying into his own soul or ours." He had "an unpretending manner," said yet another, "free of guile and affectation." One acquaintance of later years caught the subtlety of Brooks the man: "You felt you did not get into the inner citadel of his soul in any conversation. . . . But you got there when you made no effort, and were there sometimes when you did not realize it."[19] Even if he was not as reclusive as he sometimes appeared, the favored son learned to protect himself at an early age. As one of his biographers perceptively commented, "The shy boyish restraint was to mature into an adult reserve whose inner secrets Brooks alone was ever to know."[20]

The subject of attitudes toward sexual development in pre-Freudian America, and particularly Brooks's attitudes in young manhood, will be dealt with more fully later in this study. For the moment, it is enough to say that he spoke of sexual awakening in adolescence generally and indirectly. "Your grown up boy is wise in bad things," he judged, "which he used to know nothing about." There was that "murky atmosphere of passion that we have to go through."[21] He confided forthrightly in his diary that sexual desires came "creeping in thief-like in the dark night or busy day, when no one can see or no one will notice." Still, he came to the conclusion that if these desires "come frankly up and strike boldly at our door, and bid us admit them and welcome them for the message they bring, . . . ready to prove kindred to other thoughts which we have taken to our heart in other days, then we may take them by the hand and lead them in and grow stronger for their presence."[22] Those thieves seldom changed their crafty ways, he remarked, a theme to which he returned in March 1865: "And not only in our weakest points, but at our weakest times does the special attack always seem to come." It was, he declared, "very startling and bewildering sometimes to find the chance of sin occurring just when we are weakest to resist it."[23] A stain is left upon the heart "of which nobody but the man knows anything." Worse, it "gives all their unhappiness to the other stains, the debased motives, the low desires, the wicked passions of the inner life."[24] What gave him in the future a measure of comfort, as he remarked in 1888, was the knowledge that "long before I cared for Him, He cared for me; that while I wandered up and down in carelessness, perhaps while I was plunging into flagrant sin, God's eye was never off me for a moment."[25]

While in theological school Brooks wrote some mildly erotic poetry (see pp. 60–61). What evidence we possess of his pubertal changes show Victorian uneasiness with sexuality, a desire to control raw physical passions, and a discomfort with eroticism.[26] But, unlike some other male diarists in nineteenth-century America, he did not omit the subject of sex, nor was his language that of total sexual denial. Freud believed that excessive sexual self-restraint produces neurotic suffering and "well-mannered weaklings." Neither applies here. Brooks was well mannered, but he also had the commanding presence of strength. What he said about preaching in his Yale lectures he meant to extend as well to the individual: "Be frank, brave, simple."[27] The advice was as truly self-revelatory as it was unself-conscious and not the attitude of one who is fearful. Freud also judged that "the relationship between possible sublimation and necessary sexual activity naturally fluctuates sharply among individuals."[28]

In this case it is not possible for the biographer to satisfy the curious in regard to Brooks's sexual activity. The man is not here to be questioned; but if he were, he might prove as recalcitrant in giving the answers we want as William James was in revealing to his generation whether or not he believed in God. (On that subject James remained firmly and politely mum. To have done otherwise would have diverted attention from what he had to say about the *will* to believe and the varieties of religious experience.) Similarly, Brooks would have seen no purpose in writing autobiographically about his sex life. Defining people by their sexual preference, as our age does, would not have been particularly interesting to him and probably very puzzling. That he never married is a fact. That he did indeed express himself in young manhood on the subject of the relation between men and women remains to be discussed.

Whatever the details, the boy at the Boston Latin School was not afraid of his body. If, as a young person, he was not sure of his poetic powers, he took personal satisfaction about both his mental abilities and his physical size and appearance. There was also an added dimension of inspiration called Spirit:

> Well, call them failures, if you will,
> These lines I wrote, these words I said;
> For me there lives a Spirit still
> That stirs the pulses of the dead.
>
> They show at least how stage by stage
> My manhood grew from less to more,
> Achieving thought with ripening age,
> And wisdom all unguessed before.
>
> I watch them as I watch the wall,
> Whereon, a boy that would be man,

> I scored my waxing height on all
> My birthdays since the wish began.[29]

Exuberant and immodest lines, yet by the time he was fourteen Brooks stood 5'11" tall, though he weighed only 133 pounds. He rejoiced in that large frame to which his family, as we have seen, drew attention.[30] Growth—physical, intellectual, and moral—was a reiterated theme.[31] In 1877, again in the Yale lectures on preaching, he urged students: "*be vital, be alive, not dead.* Do everything that can keep your vitality at its fullest. Even the physical vitality do not dare to disregard." He knew a preacher who "seems to me to have a large part of his power simply in his physique, in the impression of vitality, in the magnetism almost like a material thing."[32] He might have been describing himself.

If Brooks learned the basic academic disciplines at Boston Latin, it was within the family circle first, and then at Harvard College, that he was introduced to the wider worlds of English and German literature that were becoming increasingly influential in America.[33] At home, both parents and children read poetry aloud in the back parlor—often with prose works as well: Robert and Elizabeth Browning, Shakespeare, Cowper, and Dickens, to name a few of the more prominent.

By the 1850s, Harvard had begun offering students more varied intellectual courses than were available when disgruntled students had attacked college property, blowing up parts of buildings in 1834 and 1842.[34] Since then the college had become the "Headquarters of Good Principles." When Brooks entered the freshman class in 1852 at the age of fifteen, Harvard had only 304 students enrolled. In his first two years Brooks did not branch out into new fields but continued to pursue the classics. He read Plato, Xenophon's "Memorabilia" of Socrates, Aeschylus and Sophocles among the Greek authors, and Cicero, Horace, Seneca, and Tacitus among the Latin. All standard fare. His highest marks were in Greek, which by then he read for pleasure. But he began also to take both French and German, and the latter soon became a favorite language with him. Indeed, he excelled in languages. He also did very well on examinations.

There appears to have been abundant leisure time for nomadic reading in biography, poetry, criticism (literary and later biblical), and novels. Brooks read rapidly and took full advantage of the opportunity, thereby setting a pattern for the rest of his life. But his class standing suffered accordingly, if not conspicuously. In his freshman year he stood sixth out of sixty-six classmates; in his sophomore year he stood sixteenth; thereafter he was thirteenth. During his last two years he began to explore English and American literature, again on his own time, since there was no English department at Harvard. He enjoyed the English Civil War royalist Richard Lovelace, as well as Dryden, Swift, Sir Walter Scott, Irving, Emerson, Tennyson—the great essayist of the human comedy—Montaigne, and Boswell (especially his *Life of Samuel Johnson*.)[35] And still the classics, this time the second century A.D. Greek satirist Lucian. It was a curious mixture of the romantic and the skeptic, not unlike Brooks's own personality. As Alexander V. G. Allen noted, there was in the young New Englander a "spirit of mockery" and raillery that seemed Rabelaisian. In photographs taken while he was at Harvard, Brooks first appears stolid and full-lipped; then increasingly there is an air of detachment, of cool grace, even hauteur. But, as Allen concluded, beneath the young man's demeanor lay "a deeper seriousness, the sense of the seriousness of life—that feeling which he had inherited from Puritan ancestors—too deeply ingrained a mood to be overcome."[36] No doubt the mocking tone was a defense, partly his own and naturally come by; but it was partly also because the moment in the mid-1850s in America when he was struggling to become an adult was, as we shall see, a critical and bewildering time.

Brooks nonetheless threw himself with enthusiasm into life at Harvard. He was a member of an exceptional class at the college. Among his friends were Edward Barry Dalton (his roommate), who became a famous Civil War surgeon and, in the last year of the war, was in charge of all the hospitals of the Army of the Potomac. Later, in New York City, Dalton organized the first city ambulance system in the nation. Francis Channing Barlow, another friend, went on to become a gallant major general with the Army of the Potomac and saw continuous service from Antietam to Spotsylvania, where his troops captured four thousand Confederate soldiers and two generals. Barlow later became the attorney general of New York and prosecuted the Tweed Ring. As a member of the undergraduate Natural History Society during his college days, Brooks came to know Alexander Agassiz, son of the famed Louis Agassiz and himself a deep-sea explorer and eventually curator of the Museum of Comparative

Zoology at Harvard. Agassiz was joined by another classmate and fellow naturalist, Theodore Lyman, a Union soldier, marine scientist, and member of Congress. Franklin B. Sanborn, another friend, eventually became a journalist, editor of the *Boston Commonwealth* and the *American Journal of Social Science,* secretary of the Massachusetts Board of Charities, and one of the founders of the National Prison Association and the Concord Summer School of Philosophy. Sanborn wrote biographies of a raft of luminaries, among them Emerson, Thoreau, Hawthorne, Samuel Gridley Howe, and William Ellery Channing. Another classmate who became a newspaperman was C. A. Chase, future editor of Boston's *Daily Advertiser.* Brooks's closest friend was George C. Sawyer, who, after a few years at Phillips Exeter Academy, went on to become for forty years the successful headmaster of the Utica Free Academy. E. H. Abbot, Brooks's rival at the Boston Latin School, taught at the equally prestigious Dixwell School in Boston.[37]

Besides the Natural History Society, Brooks was elected to other college clubs and organizations: in his freshman year, the Institute of 1770; the Hasty Pudding Club in his sophomore year; in his junior year, the literary society Alpha Delta Phi; and finally, as a senior, Phi Beta Kappa.[38] But neither he nor his classmates appear to have taken any of these clubs with great seriousness. He never participated in the religious society on campus, called the Christian Brethren. In 1855, his class, brilliant above the average and not content with these social and literary offerings, founded The Anonyma, a debating society.[39]

Nineteenth-century Americans went in droves to hear lectures, debates, and sermons—much as people today partake of salad bars. Educated males were expected to be able to deliver speeches, contend in forensics, and edify with disquisitions; the sermons of ministers were meant to instruct and illuminate. Each, it was expected, would be accompanied by the graces of appropriate intonation and gesture. (Gentlewomen, except Quakers, were not supposed to speak in public at all.[40]) With his ability to read rapidly and express himself clearly, Brooks was often called on to deliver papers at meetings of the undergraduate societies of which he was a member. No doubt others were as well. In his case, the thoughts he expressed anticipated his future attitudes to a remarkable degree. Several broad themes emerge from these student compositions: communication, social class, the interpretation of history, and religion.

In "The Lecturer," a paper he read in his freshman year before the Institute of 1770, Brooks applauded the role of the lecturer. The speaker's subject, he declared, was not as important as the fact that he is an oracle: "It is the manner & matter of the lecturer's speech that go to make up the effect, for the lecturer's aim is to teach not so much by imparting mere facts as to the pregnant suggestiveness of his thoughts." He must make his audience "feel with him & with the changes of his feeling they must change." The good lecturer is a sort of "magician . . . with all the powers of drama at his hand." While Brooks came to despise elocution and the flowery Victorian delivery that often went with it, he understood that the lecturer—and later the preacher—"raises the curtain & shows his auditors the stage of life with all its characters."[41] In later life he would raise the curtain on the biblical world and invite his parishioners to walk a terrain not unlike their own. It is worth noting that he was not drawn to abstract thought but to the world of people and events. To his credit, he believed that one could be dramatic and remain simple at the same time.

On 13 July 1853, in another speech before the Institute of 1770, Brooks turned his attention to social class. In this address he took notice of three classes in society: "These are 1st the Laboring Classes (so-called), 2ndly The Literary Classes (the term being taken in its widest sense) & 3rd the Aristocratic Classes (also understood in their most extended meaning)." While he suggested that some would not find a place in any of the three, still there are generally the "Handworkers, the Headworkers, [and the] No-workers."[42]

Brooks associated himself with the "literary class," which had "recently felt sympathy for those below them." Laboring people "are beginning to find friends in the talented, refined & polished," he judged. In what was no doubt an oblique reference to Dickens and possibly to Harriet Beecher Stowe, he went on to say that the "oppressed and degraded . . . the white slaves in the old world & black slaves in the new & the poor white freemen in both have each been made the theme of the writer & amelioration of their condition his aim." About the aristocratic class he was less complimentary and referred to the "fancied preeminence" of its members. He rejected the aristocracies of strength, of wealth, and of birth. Of the latter he remarked in a nice turn of phrase, if the aristocrat "be poor, he wraps himself snugly up in his coat of arms." Brooks found only the "aristocracy of merit" to his liking, for it alone "is free from pride or at least from all unlawful pride, an aristocracy which is truly *best* & which seeks to raise rather than crush its inferiors." The others he considered arbitrary. But he seriously weakened his argument by declaring, naïvely, that "refinement and education" will "soften and instruct" the upper classes. "Besides," he concluded, "it is absolutely necessary that the Laboring Classes should have something above them in social position to which they may look up for example in the minor duties & decencies of life." The Declaration of Independence's notion, he determined, that "All men are Created Equal . . . is a doctrine disproved by every birth, . . . tried [by utopians] & found impractical." Each class, he thought, was needed and had its own duties to perform—an ambiguous statement marked at best by noblesse oblige.[43]

In 1854, Brooks addressed the Hasty Pudding Club on the subject of "Man and His World." This paper was the reworking of a theme written the year before that bore the more intriguing title "National Greetings & Sports as Hints of National Character."[44] His Hasty Pudding presentation provided an interpretation of the history of western European civilization from a Protestant and American perspective. While the prejudices expressed tell us hardly anything of historical value, they reveal much about their purveyor.

Like not a few others then and since, Brooks looked back to a golden, classical period when "the world was young, [and] everything was fresh & manners with the rest." Feelings and emotions were indicated by natural, simple "motions and gestures." Bowing the head and bending the knee were "intuitive of all marks of respect." It was no anachronism in Milton, he declared, "to represent our first parents, blessed with total uncivilization, as *kneeling* in prayer on the first morning of their joint existence, for it is no mere conventional usage but something which man brings with him."[45]

As manners were simple, so in the Old Testament was religion. Then—Brooks was blissfully vague on the date—came "refinement and elaboration . . . till feeling was swallowed up in expression." Artificiality came to dominate the civilized world "under the hot sun of the East." Medieval Crusaders brought Eastern manners to Europe, and the "flowery, showy scion of Shem took strength and flourished in the seed of Japhet." As a result of such baneful influences, he added, the high Middle Ages displayed a "great deal of learning and a great deal of folly." It would have surprised Muslims to have had medieval scholasticism laid at their door, but Brooks was undaunted. Both philosophy and science, he suggested, were dominated by argument, not by empirical observation. Intellectual and social ostentation came from the "hot blood of the East." Moreover, the "priest-ridden, luxurious, diseased & bloated courts of the middle ages[,] . . . the delirious craving for the artificial," in turn produced monks, monasteries, saints, and superstitions.[46]

Brooks believed that by studying the "complicated forms of chivalry, elaborate pantomimes of the Romans, . . . the Morris dances of the English; [and the] ballet dances of the French," it was possible to detect a movement from the simple to the elaborate and then, in the third stage of civilization, back to the simple. That third stage, in which he placed his own time, was characterized by the "renewing of Simplicity." But for a time the world's "two best physicians, plain Common Sense & true Religion[,] almost abandoned their patient in despair . . . [as a result of] his delirious craving for the artificial."[47] There was no doubt where Brooks stood, though the price of adopting such an interpretation was high. It meant ignoring contemporary German church historians and the Oxford Movement, let alone the Gothic revival in America. These hardly disturbed the assurance and tranquility of Brooks's very Protestant interpretation, however. But the explication serves to describe the man himself.

His final college paper, dated 17 July 1855, was less culturally and more personally revealing. "The Huguenot Preacher" is in fact a kind of testament to his own faith. Brooks chose as his subject Paul Rabaut, the eighteenth-century French pastor of "the Church in the Desert." Rabaut, a bold and persevering diplomat, strove to obtain civil rights for Protestants in France. He became, to the young American, a hero who "grasp[ed] the *Present* to see the Good of his own wretched age." Rabaut "lived and preached among poor, wretched Huguenots . . . in the South of France." He also lived in a time of declining faith when "in the salons of Paris the Philosophy of the 18th century, with its great apostles Diderot, Helvetius, D'Alembert, was clearing the way for the Revolution." Still, amid this "desperate tangle," Rabaut did not lose heart. Instead, he "traced the bright golden thread of his Belief, running unbroken & unharmed through the whole." Even the persecution of his people gave this champion of French Protestants "life and vigor." Brooks wrote: "Through the faith that clothed his life, he [Rabaut] looked at all the life around him & saw it the clearer & better for the faith."[48]

The Frenchman understood events and possibilities for what they were and, at the same time, "through a kind of glory" that sprang from his religion. As a result, Rabaut stood like some Old Testament prophet, warning the philosophers "around their table that they were ruining themselves and France." If there were greater minds in the century than that of this Huguenot pastor, Brooks judged, "there was not one greater man." Then he came to a telling conclusion: "These are the lives that teach the world to live. . . . [They] stand along the streets of daily life, looking quietly down like strong statues upon the business . . . and the works of the world . . . perpetuating their Faith forever."[49] In his desire to see black Americans achieve their political rights, in his maintenance of faith in an age that questioned faith's assumptions, and in his optimistic moralism, Brooks reflected the qualities he perceived in Paul Rabaut.[50]

Brooks clearly meant to emulate the likes of such people. He would be a public man, not a scholar, one close to the everyday style and passions of ordinary human beings. In "Man and His World," he used the metaphor of a library to describe the people he observed around him. On the lower shelves were the "great, ponderous tomes for study," which he judged, unfairly, were "full of dullness, decency & dust." On the top shelves were the lighter works, "sometimes attractive, often pleasing but always of passing interest & fleeting worth." In the middle were those books that he prized, books that were "strong, earnest, popular, pleasing specimens of Life and Literature."[51] Such was his daily fare.

A middle-class Victorian without aristocratic pretensions, an American Protestant strongly attracted to the reformed faith, Brooks was a young man with a wide cultural and literary background and interests. He expected to make his mark and to command the respect of his contemporaries. Sure of his background and of his ability, he was content to be who he was. And, one suspects, the same was true of many of his classmates at Harvard in the 1850s.

Brooks probably read more widely than some. Certainly in the period of personal crisis that, as we shall see, went from the late fall of 1855 to October 1856, he sought refuge and enlightenment in the works of Elizabeth Browning, Shelley, Goethe, and, to a lesser degree, Milton, Coleridge, and Wordsworth. In the meantime, while still an undergraduate, he found another hero to place alongside Rabaut. Amid all the volumes Brooks consumed in college, there was one book that made a profound impression on him: Thomas Carlyle's *Life and Letters of Oliver Cromwell* (1845). This biography opened up the seventeenth century for him, and he went on to read Milton—the starting point for the Romantics—Richard Baxter, and Jeremy Taylor. Later in life he yearned to write his own biography of Cromwell.[52] Though not a historian, Carlyle created in Brooks, as he did in others, a keen interest in the names associated with the Puritan struggle. From *Cromwell* and from Boswell's *Johnson,* the young American came to search for figures who struck him as worthy examples of what appeared to be the best in human accomplishment or, in some cases, embodiments of divine revelation itself. His earlier readings of Scott, Longfellow, Irving, and Tennyson also contributed to hero worship, a penchant that was surely the temper of the times. In pursuing his heroes, Brooks sought a ground for value, for an aesthetic, and, above all, for an identity that would not give way beneath his feet. Nietzsche had not yet denied the very existence of that ground and declared that value and identity were illusions.[53]

There were nonetheless characteristics in Brooks's personality that were compensatory, even countervailing, to his hero worship. These appeared when, in his last year in college (1855), he was again asked by his peers to read a paper at the Hasty Pudding Club on the eighteenth-century English politician and letter writer Horace Walpole. Brooks noted the man's limitations and went on to suggest, gratuitously, that "greatness and goodness both require something greater and better than the mere selfish life of the courtier or a man of taste to work themselves out in."[54] It was a forgivable, if regrettable, bit of sanctimony in a twenty-year-old.[55] But then, in the approaching June of senior year, he could afford to be less ponderous.

In a more spontaneous mood, Brooks wrote to his eldest brother, on the eve of graduation in 1855, "Yessiree! One week more & we're through College, Educated Men & then, look out for the consequences. Lord! Won't the old world open its eyes when it sees the Class of '55 coming from Cambridge like a whirlwind." He had in his possession, he told William, the "chrystalotypes of his class & they are beyond dispute the ugliest looking set of eighty men that could be selected from the country." He wished his brother, who was in Chicago, could come to class day "& then we'd have a party up here & a good time generally." As it was, he mused, "I shall probably not have a soul but roaming about all day like a wandering Spirit in a white vest, looking on and doing most nothing." Then he lamented, "It's going to cost us ten dollars apiece."[56] Four years later, he exhibited the same animation when his younger brothers Frederick and Arthur proved to be "medal scholars" and winners of the Boylston Prize at Harvard: "What's up in Boston?" he inquired again of William. "Has the town recovered from the shock of those pigs [prizes] the Brooks boys carried off?"[57]

Though he was the one who carried off the lion's share of the "prizes," Phillips Brooks wanted others to have access to them as well. Later in life he declared at a girls' school that "all great ends of education . . . know no limit and no coloring of sex. . . . To all women, as to all men, beckon the great ambitions of prophet, philosopher, worker, and saint." Womens' lives were drawn too narrowly, he believed. "The knowledge of arithmetic or cookery is not 'more practical' than knowledge of eclipses or Greek verbs, or the wonders of rocks or of ancient histories."[58]

3

Failure and the Poetry of Heroics

When young people reach the "defining moment" in a period of historical crisis, they often become marked for the rest of their lives by the pervading spirit of those months or years. This was particularly true of youth during the Great Depression. At that time there was a strange combination, in America at least, of economic fear and political optimism—an equation that was reversed in the 1950s. Nowhere, perhaps, was the personal defining moment more starkly etched against the background of cultural disillusionment than in Weimar Germany after World War I. Ulrich Hoever speaks of the failure of expectations German youth experienced in the early 1920s and, as a consequence, "their rejection of rationality and objectivity, their penchant for the 'daemonic,' for ecstasy and delirium, for despair and vitalism, for surrender to feeling and readiness for action."[1] Only in the late 1960s and early 1970s did American youth come close to the experience of Germans.

In the decade before the Civil War, Americans found their society disintegrating. Many, like Edward Everett, discovered, as George B. Forgie points out, "that the world [they] had always known was becoming unrecognizable." Conservatives, among them William G. Brooks, Sr., who were primarily interested in social calm, order, and business profits rather than "the rights of slaves, slaveholders, or free labor, tended to be people who by temperament shrank from the unpleasantness of invective and the tumble of political life that grew ever more desperate."[2] The elder Brooks confided in his diary in October 1860 that "we are fallen upon hard & evil times, hardly clear of the panic of 1857 & certainly not recovered from it before we are upon another & serious one." This time the panic "is a political one but [it] operates financially. . . . it affects the business operations of the whole country."[3] Even more important, but only dimly seen by William Brooks, was the new political alignment, the Civil War party system, which in the 1850s replaced the failed presidencies of three colorless, proslavery northerners: Millard Fillmore, Franklin Pierce, and James Buchanan.

Disillusionment with the nation had arisen within the span of a decade. American society was shaken by the passage of the Compromise of 1850, or Omnibus Act (which contained the famous fugitive slave provision); by the fateful acceptance of the Kansas-Nebraska Act of 1854, which repealed the Missouri Compromise of 1820 and brought on bloody clashes between pro- and antislavery settlers; by Chief Justice Roger Taney's opinion in *Dred Scott v. Sandford* (1857) that Congress had no power to prohibit slavery in the territories; and ultimately by the possibility that the courts might subsequently strike down antislavery constitutions in free states. As Kenneth Stampp has noted, there was widespread and acute foreboding among whites of slave rebellion in the South. In the North, the huge influx of immigrants (2½ million in the 1850s), which peaked just prior to 1857, created an upsurge in antiforeign sentiment. As a result, distrust of strangers and that peculiar brand of xenophobia, Know-Nothingism, charged the atmosphere, as Bostonites and other city dwellers forgot that they too had once been immigrants. Increasing lawlessness, police corruption, counterfeiting, and armed burglaries plagued the cities.[4]

In the religious communities in the 1850s both theological prejudices and sectional rivalries tore denominations apart. In general, Protestants thought what was Protestant was American, while Catholics did not discriminate between pietistic revivals and anti-Catholic crusades. Those coming out of the Puritan heritage seemed to Catholics to be the most bigoted of all Protestants. As a result, Irish Americans were unenthusiastic about abolition, while in the Protestant churches of the North there was a rising tide of social action against slavery. The growing fervor among Protestant leaders, writes James Moorhead, "roused from somnolent optimism large numbers of clergy."[5] As a young theological student, Phillips Brooks was caught up with them in that tide. Along with other newly minted abolitionists, he joined the Republican party, confiding in his elder brother that he could not believe their father had voted for Fillmore in the election of 1856.[6] His contempt for Buchanan was equally palpable. Lewis Cass, Robert Augustus Toombs, John Jordan Crittenden, Steven A. Douglas, even William Henry Seward failed to impress him when he visited the Senate chamber early in 1857.[7] Such negative opinions were part of a general disillusionment with government by those who felt that the cohesion of the nation was at risk and that the democratic experiment was on the brink of failure. No doubt that fear accounts in part for Brooks's self-imposed isolation and acerbic remarks during his first two years at the Episcopal Theological Seminary in Virginia.

If, in joining the Republican party, Brooks distanced himself from business-as-usual politics, he also stood apart from many popular customs and manners that were evolving in the 1850s. At that time a new theatricality made its appearance in dress, deportment, church architecture, and ecclesiastical ritual. Theatricality was a way of hiding divisions and disillusionment—perhaps even fear—behind a mask of manners. Karen Halttunen notes the fading in the 1840s of the "sentimental demand for sincerity in dress," with its roots in American Puritanism and, increasingly in the 1850s, the greater willingness "to accept dress as a form of disguise."[8] For his part, Brooks disliked theatricality and the drama of disguise; he even held something of an aversion for the theater itself, with its "histrionic art . . . [that] demanded for success weakness rather than strength of character." In matters of dress he was neat and unostentatious. When he traveled, he did so, as a Scottish clergyman remarked, "'in the garb of what seemed like a well-to-do gamekeeper.'"[9]

Brooks "disliked affected manners" and once exclaimed, "If only people would be simple!" As to opulence, he spoke disparagingly on occasion of the rich who "flung their money about." By the decade of the 1850s, the yardstick of personal worth, it has been suggested, was taste rather than virtue, display rather than constraint. "Most important," Brooks noted, "the sentimental dread of hypocrisy was yielding to a new appreciation for the aesthetic value of personal disguise."[10] Clearly, he embraced the simplicity and directness of the earlier generation.

He stood apart in other ways as well. Along with growing opulence and ostentation, Christian attitudes were, it has been claimed, adapted and trivialized to fit the customs of social intercourse. "Etiquette advisers," John Kasson reminds us, "never tired of insisting that the basis of politeness was the Golden Rule, and that the epitome of the gentleman was Jesus."[11] To be sure, Christian meekness remained, but it was required of Jesus' mid-century followers "in the form of modesty" in conversation, not of patience under injury. Christian peace "was demanded as social harmony, Christian self-denial as a polite forgetfulness of self, and Christian trust was insisted upon as that 'confidence in the good intentions of our neighbors' which 'makes society possible.'"[12] Such trivialization held little appeal for Brooks. As we shall see, besides his desire to get to the heart of Christian faith, he felt that his sense of irony and "his power of satire, . . . withering when he gave it full scope," had to be restrained. But satire feeds on the banalities and hypocracies of behavior, and Brooks loved "clear, simple humor . . . and had a rippling way of describing ludicrous scenes."[13] Such a person is not likely to fit closely held beliefs to the customs of social relations but to judge social relations from the vantage point of belief.

Church architecture in the 1850s paralleled the new pretensions in dress. It was the era, according to James F. White, of the mature years of the Ecclesiological Society in England and of the triumph of the gothic revival.[14] Walker Gwynne gave perhaps unwitting testimony to the new self-conscious triumphalism of much American Gothic architecture when he spoke of the New York [Ecclesiological] Society as "the beginning in America of *real* Church architecture, liturgical science, and their allied arts of ornamentation and music."[15] That the church built for Phillips Brooks—Trinity Church, on Copley Square—was decidedly not Gothic is itself significant of the independence of those who built it, including the rector. Trinity's Spanish Romanesque style was a deliberate choice.

In terms of church customs and manners, Brooks, as we have seen already, avoided "every badge of clerical dress."[16] Along with new rules for deportment at theaters, concerts, and dinner tables that began in the 1850s,[17] church deportment appeared for the first time in etiquette manuals. How to enter church, sit, pray, listen, and exit, writes Halttunen, "demanded a demeanor of restrained piety, genteel performance of religious reverence."[18] The rituals of funerals and of mourning were increasingly "coming to resemble a form of public theatre, in which the performances not only of the mourners but of the corpse itself became the object of open and unabashedly theatrical concern."[19] But Brooks showed little interest in such matters. When a nervous gentleman wondered aloud at a wedding rehearsal what he should do after escorting the bride down the aisle, he was cheerfully told, "'Anything you please; nobody will care.'"[20] Brooks was equally capable of waving aside the social canons of polite society. When the scrubwoman at Trinity Church diffidently asked if her daughter could be married in the chapel, the rector replied, "'Why not take the church?'" When she responded, "'But that is not for the likes of me,'" he declared, "'Oh yes, it *is* for the likes of *you,* and the likes of *me,* and the likes of every one.'"[21] With such freedom he dismissed what appeared to him to be trivialities and false solemnities.

But Brooks was going against convention. As with both public deportment and the architectural styling of churches, prescribed ceremonial for the clergy and "expertise" in the conduct of ritual were greatly enhanced with the publication in 1848 of the *Hierugia Anglicana; or, Documents and Extracts Illustrative of the Ritual of the Church in England after the Reformation.*[22] Studied ceremonial manners replaced spontaneity. William Augustus Muhlenberg made the Church of the Holy Communion in New York City the center of the new ritualism of the 1850s. As one graduate of the nearby General Theological Seminary recalled: "Our highest exponent of ceremonial and ritual was the Church of the Holy Communion, then considered the extremest height possible, and its extremes consisted of a proper altar with a cross and flowers, and a choir of unvested boys who chanted the Psalter."[23] Donald M. Scott has discerned that the more evangelical churches were not by any means immune to the new theatricality and that "increasingly the preacher had become a performer, and the service itself . . . a special kind of performance which engulfed the audience much as the performance of a good actor or musician would."[24] In setting, ceremony, and homily, the church became theater.

In the meantime, the seeds of the ritual controversy were being sown. Like the debate over the Oxford Movement in the 1840s, the issue of "ritualism" from the late 1860s to the middle 1870s nearly tore the Episcopal church apart.[25] From these developments, Brooks simply stood aside, though he was quite aware of what was going on around him. When a fellow clergyman whom he admired and who was a so-called ritualist expounded all the points of difference that separated them, he listened patiently. When the man was done, Brooks responded with feigned ingenuousness, "'It has all been very interesting, and I haven't understood a word of what you have been saying.'"[26]

In summary, during the 1850s the middle and upper classes were learning to distinguish between Christian trust based on sincerity and bourgeois social confidence acted out according to social forms. They opted for the latter. "They were learning to place confidence," concludes Halttunen, "not in the sincere countenance but in the social mask; to trust not in simple dress but in elaborate disguise."[27] That disguise could hide what was dangerous to face. But given the tensions of the period, that was perhaps understandable. Still, these developments were not Brooks's way.

National divisions also added an unwelcome dimension to the politics of the Episcopal church. Northern Evangelical Episcopalians increasingly separated themselves from their fellow Evangelicals in the South.[28] Especially in Virginia, where the denomination's major Evangelical seminary was located, tension between northern and southern students, as well as with the surrounding neighbors, became acute. When young northern Evangelicals gravitated toward the Republican party, the split deepened. But that was not all. Along with the slaveholders on their list of demons, Yankee Evangelicals in the Episcopal church included high-church Tractarians. The avatars of the Oxford Movement were considered enemies of traditional order in both church and state. Diana Butler describes the Evangelicals' suspicion that "both the church and their country were being dictated to by powerful, aristocratic and non-democratic minorities—Tractarians and slaveholders—whose agendas could destroy Christian and political liberty." As a result, northern low churchmen were in a bind: If they repudiated their southern friends, they opened "the way for the increased influence and power of Tractarianism."[29]

Already by 1858 in the American Episcopal church, one bishop and more than thirty clergy had become Roman Catholics as a result of the high-church Oxford revival. The Evangelical bishop Charles McIlvaine "believed that such conversions were part of a Roman Catholic plot to subvert the ministry of the Episcopal Church."[30] Indeed, the possibility of an "unstoppable hemorrhage" of clergy and laity worried Evangelicals deeply and drove many into closer fellowship with those of other Protestant denominations. One result of this sense of declension in the denomination was a general heightening of pietistic prayer meetings in the revival of 1857. At the Virginia Theological Seminary the revival became particularly fervent in an effort to bridge the growing divisions in church and state. For a brief time it was thought that through an upsurge of piety differences could be papered over and schism avoided. Sentiment might heal what debate could not. It was an insubstantial and evanescent notion.

Brooks's struggle to achieve independent identity was played out against the background of these national and religious tensions, which only served to make more difficult the problem of the emergence into adulthood of a gifted young man. There was, by contrast, as George Fredrickson has noted, intense pressure for commitment that drew people's attention beyond their personal lodestar.[31] At the same time, to compound the difficulty of establishing one's independence, there was a "collapse of faith in the ability of 'external' institutions to express unique points of view."[32] Both the pressure to take a stand and the failure of time-honored institutions to give direction made it difficult for university and theological students to study in an undisturbed manner, and church people were doubly distracted. The inability of Episcopalians to make up their minds at mid-century whether their cherished episcopacy was divine, plausible, or both confused everyone. As Robert Bruce Mullin has stated, the "intraepiscopal furor that raged for much of the 1840s and that entailed long trials and acrid debates deeply troubled Episcopalians from all points of the compass."[33]

Threatened with a decline in orthodoxy in what was also an intensely religious decade, people sought to express their inward religious convictions in loyalty to their inherited traditions. They were hard-pressed to do so. They could not—or chose not to—escape into a merely private spirituality; and many felt as well that they could no longer live in a nominal, public one. Some objective center, writes Richard Rabinowitz, where "a magical intimacy between mindfulness and godliness" could be expressed, must be found.[34] Phillips discovered that center, but it was a long and painful journey.

· · ·

In the summer of 1855 Phillips Brooks was a nineteen-year-old college graduate in need of a job. His standing as a student as well as his academic interests pointed toward teaching, ultimately in a college. To gain experience as well as make a living, he applied to the Boston Latin School for a position and was accepted. He joined the faculty of his alma mater as an usher (assistant teacher). If he did well teaching school, he thought, in a few years he could go abroad, probably to Germany, for an advanced degree. In the meantime, teaching Latin and Greek to schoolboys was good experience and a safe course. The circumscribed world of Boston and Cambridge held for him only familiar faces, well-known scenes, and foreseeable demands. He could live at home, be well fed, and, according to his brother William, seat his now 204 pounds in "the chair alongside the sideboard at prayers . . . [and in] the comfortable rocking chair" in the back parlor.[35] He might also finally make the decision to be confirmed at St. Paul's Church, though he was by no means sure he would take that step. He had never had a conversion experience—and never would.[36] Clearly, he had not chosen a particularly adventurous path.

At first, all went well at Boston Latin. Brooks taught the younger boys with patience and kindness. Since he himself had never needed severe discipline as an incentive to study, he gave no thought to disciplining others. His first charges were as inoffensive as their teacher. But in the middle of October the headmaster, Francis Gardner, suddenly reassigned him to a class of boys ranging in age from fifteen to seventeen. These students, to whom he was supposed to teach French, Greek, and Latin (Virgil), had already proved to be disciplinary problems. They had "ambushed" three teachers and routed them from the school. For Gardner's part, putting a nineteen-year-old in such a position was not only cruel but vindictive—the headmaster personally disliked his newest usher. As Phillips's cousin and friend in college, Charles Francis Adams, Jr., remarked, Gardner tended to play favorites. To those he liked he showed a kindly side, but to "those he did not like a harder and less charitable man it would not be easy to find." Adams went on to say that anyone who knew both men "would feel instinctively at once that Francis Gardner could never have taken kindly to Phillips Brooks."[37]

Confusion reigned in Brooks's new classroom. According to Raymond Albright, he was "overconfident in their [the students'] interest in learning." They "locked him in his room, scattered explosive matches on the classroom floor, and even threw a handful of buckshot in his face."[38] Brooks was sick at heart, cross, tired, and, worst of all, as he wrote to his friend George C. Sawyer, ashamed.[39] It was not the first time he had confronted failure. In his next to last year as a student at Boston Latin, he did not receive top prizes in Latin, mathematics, or poetry, as had been expected. Instead, his classmate Edwin H. Abbott marched off with most of the academic laurels, and Brooks was stunned. A year later he graduated third in his class when he had expected to be first.[40] Again Abbott was ahead of him.

But Brooks's teaching failure was different. Here there was no middle ground, no satisfaction of work finely, but not supremely, done. As a result, he hated himself *and* his students. He became confused, made a mistake, and punished a boy who had committed no wrong. He began to lose confidence in himself. To "Top" Sawyer, who was teaching successfully at Exeter,[41] he had earlier remarked, "if you meet a Latin School boy you will at once know him for one who . . . knows ever so much, probably a good deal more than his master." Even some of his younger charges, he wrote, were "pretty sharp and have come very near sticking me very often on strange rules in out-of-the-way corners of the grammar of whose existence I was profoundly ignorant." But with that first class he was able to fall back on the "*ipse dixit* of a schoolmaster."[42] Not so with the older class. Of its thirty-five members he wrote in December 1855: "*They are the most disagreeable set of creatures without exception that I have ever met with.*"[43] However, by January he was able to confide to his patient friend, "Things have settled down into a strong feeling of quiet hate, which is eminently conducive to good order and rapid progress." Still, he knew of no teacher who was "honored with such an overwhelming share of deep, steady, honest unpopularity as is the lot of your harmless and inoffensive friend."[44] He abruptly resigned from the school on 6 February 1856.

Brooks was, as his cousin Charles Adams judged, "humiliated, discouraged, utterly broken down, indeed by his complete failure at the threshold of life, not seeing well or at all in what direction to turn or to apply his hand." In the depth of his mortification he went to a family friend and asked if he could "suggest any way in which it would be possible for him . . . to earn a living!"[45] Two years later he recapitulated in his notebook his feelings at the time: "Up again from the dust. . . . In a sadder & soberer courage with wiser prudence & a humble heart we struggle on with . . . the banner that our cowardice flung away." There was no room for pride, he concluded, "when in our bravest struggles we look up and see . . . not only the hope of triumph but the memory of defeat."[46] Nor would he ever forget that experience at Boston Latin. But did he overreact? Was he too sensitive, lacking in perspective?[47] The events, sharp and painful, stood out in his mind. An important segment of the only society he had ever known rejected him. His own school, the very people in whose circle he had developed his skills and who he thought he understood, had in effect thrown him out. His home itself had been a schoolhouse where hymns were recited; at Harvard he had been called on to address his fellow students. Now, in his view, all of that was in jeopardy.

Shortly before Brooks left Boston Latin—in fact, it was the catalyst for his resignation—the headmaster told him—with others in earshot—that "he never knew a man who failed in teaching to succeed in anything else." It was a heartless condemnation. Before many months had passed, Brooks wrote that he preferred to think that Gardner's remark was that of the schoolmaster and not the man. Nor could he bring himself to express the anger and anguish he felt. Pretending that the condemnation had been directed to him professionally, not personally, he wrote, "I have failed myself most signally in teaching school." But, he continued, "[I] am not yet quite ready to acknowledge myself wholly unequal to all the wide world's work."[48] It was a show of courage.

At the time of his son's departure from Boston Latin, William Brooks recorded in his diary:

> An occurrence took place this week that has given us some anxiety, that of son Phillips inability to maintain his position as Usher in the Latin School. It was entirely in the want of discipline. He was not enough of a disciplinarian to maintain the necessary good order and he was put at the head of a class of 35 that were very rowdy & already had two masters [three, actually] who had left them. Not receiving the necessary assistance or advice from the Principal, I was obliged to advise his resignation. The class of boys were of 15 to 17 years of age & he but 20—the task was too much for him and he is now looking out for employment.[49]

Brooks went home and took refuge in the familial castle, "the somewhat narrow world in which I prefer to move," as he observed to his friend "Top."[50] His father lowered the portcullis, and the back parlor, "where only family members were permitted to enter uninvited," was secured.[51] When Alexander Vinton, the rector of St. Paul's, sent word for Phillips to come to see him, it was William Brooks who replied that his son would not see anyone until "after he [and, no doubt, the family] got over the feeling of mortification in consequence of his failure."[52] But Brooks never went. Instead, he called on President James Walker of Harvard. No matter that Walker was a Unitarian; Brooks respected him as a man and as an adviser.

In his self-doubt, Brooks wrote to "Top" Sawyer, a month after his resignation, "I don't think it impossible that I may give up all thoughts of teaching and go to studying my profession in the fall," adding self-mockingly, "I haven't decided what it will be."[53] In June he advised, "I wish I was fifteen years old again. I might make a stunning man, but somehow or other I don't seem in the way to come to much just now." If anything, his self-deprecation had grown. "I have not yet any possible plans for the Fall," he confessed, "but shall not study a profession. I don't exactly know what will become of me, and don't much care."[54] Later that summer he still lacked confidence in his abilities, informing his friend that "if it shall ever be in my fate to see little hungry youths around me begging for crumbs of Greek which my exhausted stock is incapable of giving, I shall know where to turn for the best supply that the country affords."[55]

Shortly thereafter, Brooks began to get out more. He went to the theater, planned to attend Harvard's midsummer commencement, and took on a few students for tutoring. Far more important, he kept on reading, this time in modern English and German literature. Insofar as he persisted in that discipline of mind to which he had been trained, he maintained a degree of balance. His reading sustained him. He engaged the authors he read, more than he had ever done before (except in the case of Carlyle). In the midst of Brooks's discouragement, the English poet Percy Bysshe Shelley provided him with the kind of heroic defiance of adverse circumstances that he desperately needed. In that highly literary age we should not be at all surprised that a poet could have such power. Brooks confided in his journal, in the summer of 1856, his admiration for Shelley's luridly anti-Christian *Queen Mab*. In that epic, Shelley loudly sang of himself for all the world to hear. He was the extravagant and impulsive hero of the poem. "Shelley at the age of 17 writing Queen Mab," declared Brooks, "seems to me, whatever we may think of the religion, the politics & ethics of that poem, to be one of the most remarkable sights we can ponder." For him Shelley "was not merely the boy of genius, like Chatterton, Byron or Keats"; he was the "boy-man with all the boy's fire and young strength & young zeal & all the man['s] earnestness of purpose & belief."[56]

Many readers will be put off by such extravagance. "The histrionic bathos of much Romantic and post-Romantic testimony as to the sublimity or terror of the lyric," writes George Steiner, "has left a dubious taste." The eloquence of Brooks's ardent response—and for that matter Shelley's—reminds us that "too many muses and angelic presences . . . have unfolded their lambent wings in too many lecture-emporia and *salons*."[57] Nonetheless, Shelley's adolescent cry of pain, his disgust with kings, priests, and merchants, his earth groaning "beneath religion's iron age" (VII.43), and his shocking travesty of the crucifixion of Jesus did not dislodge young Brooks's rather ordinary faith. Quite the contrary, it awoke in him passion and hope for the future. In Shelley's poem "A brighter morn awaits the human day, / When every transfer of material gifts / Shall be a commerce of good words and works" (V.251–53). The poet had contemplated a

> . . . high being, of cloudless brain,
> Untainted passion, elevated will,
> Which death (who even would linger long in awe
> Within his noble presence, and beneath
> His cloudless eyebeam) might alone subdue. (V.154–58)

For the Englishman's "Spirit of Nature" (I.265, III.214, 216), the American substituted the figure of Jesus Christ—it was so simple that Brooks may well have wondered why Shelley had not thought of it. There was no doubt in his mind about the Englishman's "blasphemy, for we must use the word" with respect to *Queen Mab;* but still, he wrote, "that strange poem has done more to make me a Christian than many a wise homily."[58] Shelley, to say the least, would have been surprised.

Brooks proceeded to appropriate the impulsiveness and the fire of the "mad Shelley," as he was known at Eton. Crazy or not, Shelley gave Brooks courage during his bout of depression. Brooks might have been describing himself—or what he aspired to be—when he wrote of the Englishman: "How he stands with his young face intent to seize all the converse which is ever speaking between earth and heaven . . . with all the martyr spirit of a Huss madly crying to religion & government & commerce & marriage, 'God, that you are, utter lies.'"[59]

If Shelley saw but half the truth—God in the natural order—that was a pity, as far as Brooks was concerned, for the New Englander had also found the God of Scripture and, increasingly, the God of revelation. Over the months of his late-adolescent crisis, Brooks began to bring together the faith of his childhood and the currents of Romantic thought to which he was exposed.

Shelley's myopia about the God of Christian Scripture may have been one thing to pity, but Brooks felt sorrier for the reader "who can read the poem & through all his horror at the sacrilege & disgust & disapproval of false morality, false logic, false history & false hope that fill it, not feel a thrill of honor & pity & love for the poor, pure man who wrote it." Shelley "was not content to live in the darkness as most do; he had a depth of feeling & height of genius to be what he was." Brooks liked the English poet's emphasis on the exceptional. He also came to see a purity of purpose in the poet's "love & joy religion," adding that the "purity that was within him, I take to be precisely that which is in the religion of Christ."[60] Like other Romantics then and since, Brooks confused heat and light. He went on to read the *Revolt of Islam* and *Prometheus Unbound,* enjoying "ecstatic moments of aesthetic perception."[61] Though he shared some of Shelley's mordant skepticism, unlike the poet he resolved not to remain alienated from his surroundings.

During this time Brooks also discovered Goethe, both the inspirer and the critic of the young Romantics with their "shrieks & noise." He read *Aus meinem Leben: Dichtung und Warheit,* which was of more than passing interest to him. A few years later he urged on his family George Henry Lewes's biography of the sage of Weimar.[62] A sonnet he composed to Goethe is full of allusions to the "great wise man / Ripened with slow strength from the glorious boy." Brooks also expressed approval of the master's advice to young writers: "Make me feel what I have not yet felt, make me think what I have not yet thought, then I will praise you." And he rejoiced in Goethe's lyric subjectivity, his "new experience of grief & joy, / Lending its life to unify the plan," the German's "earnest search of nature & her truth," his "kindly sympathy with humankind," and his "kingly friendship"—qualities that Brooks would attempt to emulate in his sermons and in his personal life.[63] Goethe became a hero to him, and, because of his compassion and fellow-feeling, a more important one than Shelley. Brooks declared that the German

Romantic stood with Homer and Shakespeare as one of "earth's great landmarks," a soul sent by God.[64] Goethe's Faust was also to be admired, a man who, desperately lonely within the solitude of knowledge, triumphs over the powers of evil. And so on.

Later on there would be others: Schiller, Matthew Arnold, Cousin, Longfellow, Emerson, the Brownings, Ruskin, and Lowell. Brooks was steeped in the literature of his age no less than in the Greek and Latin poets. His ability to speak the English language simply and lucidly grew out of hours of such reading. What is remarkable is that he avoided theatricality and the temptation to rhetorical display. Instead, he listened. He ascribed to the poetic, as we shall see, to the forms of meaning within language, an aesthetic potency through which "otherness" enters into our lives and "translates" us, making us part of it. Nor is such an assertion the relic of the nineteenth century. As George Steiner suggests, "It is the epic and the lyric, the tragedy and the comedy, it is the novel which exercises the most penetrative authority over our consciousness" and makes us human.[65]

James Marsh's American edition of Samuel Taylor Coleridge's *Aids to Reflection* (1829) was also as important for Brooks as it was for others of his age, beginning with Emerson himself.[66] Coleridge was indebted to Immanuel Kant's *Critique of Pure Reason,* with its distinction between understanding and reason, but he and the Americans who read Kant together with Marsh's introduction simply overlooked the philosopher's strictures on reason. Their unsystematic reading provided a means of discarding the idea of the mind's passivity, long an unexamined assumption of the Scottish Realists and their American disciples. For their part Coleridge's American followers—Brooks among them—claimed more power for reason than Kant had allowed. As Bruce Kucklick observes, those "who absorbed German views in roughest form often reduced the complexities of idealism to demarcating the functions of understanding and reason."[67] Understanding provided empirical truths about the natural order; reason was now free, they thought, to intuit the timeless truths of morality and religion. Even the understanding of nature, as with Emerson himself, was dependent on intuitive, suprarational insights. Kucklick remarks, "In this interpretation the active view of the mind and its role in creating the world was all that was authentically Kantian."[68] No matter the misreading, Kant, through Coleridge, was made to supply optimistic Americans with a vibrant and expansive role for reason. Out of his transcendental epistemology emerged a transcendent metaphysics that was subscribed to—for a while—by Brooks and others who were heirs to an English and American inattention to detail.

There was, however, a romantic spin on the new epistemology. It was not so much that the split between phenomenal (the physical) and noumenal (the mental) was overcome by questioning Kant's restriction on pure reason to phenomena and applying it to noumena as well (as did Hegel) but that the direct experience of the noumenal was enlarged by turning to feeling, sentiment, consciousness. Schleiermacher in Germany, Coleridge in England, and Marsh in America had discovered a fuller "reason" that promised to be a new way into the spiritual order. Insofar as they anticipated this new experience, they moved well beyond the confines of the Enlightenment's definition of reason. For them, reason assured a world of phenomena that, whether known or unknown, are linked together into a unity connecting them with each person's present experience. For Kant, thinking a world of objects meant ultimately that all human experience was part of a single system; all other experiences of all other people are therefore possible experiences of the individual and thus are correlated to the unity of the individual self, which in turn is related to the One. Coleridge called it "all-hang-togetherness."[69] From him Brooks learned the consubstantiality of all things as the many derive their being from the One.[70] And it was consubstantiality that provided the intellectual frame on which Brooks built the edifice of his preaching.

In ways of thinking, in assumptions—despite the Platonic idealism that underlay their thought—this was all very much a departure from the past. Philip Gura writes that Marsh's generation in New England "struggled with ideas so provocative that, often unknown to them, their theological formulations replaced the doctrinal elements of their theology with the *poetic,* thus revealing to their followers new dimensions of religious experience."[71] No longer did theologians ask if a doctrine were true; rather, they asked what it meant. Here the role of the poet was crucial. He or she was the new hero who alone could express the single system of experience. The poet did not so much create a world of meaning (Kant) as perceive by means of reason the unity and harmony—the meaning—of the world that was already there (Coleridge et al.).

In other ways some old Puritan-Calvinist assumptions were neatly shoehorned into the new aesthetics. In Brooks's mind, to be a Coleridgean theological poet was a privilege reserved for the few, the elect. Part of what happened to him during the years of his identity crisis involved achieving just such an understanding. The favorite, gifted son who had been thrown down in defeat had to pick himself up and regain his "chosenness." Duty called him to do so. Duty also prescribed that it be done in such a way as to contribute to more than his own satisfaction, that is, for the benefit of those around him. His tradition—family, faith, and cultural heritage in New England—asked him to be a public citizen rather than a private believer. It also urged him to preserve and recast the language of that tradition. As a result, election and covenant theology found themselves dressed in new, beautiful garb.

In 1859, in his last year as a theological student, Brooks gave a lecture on poetry in which he made clear "the preeminence above his fellows" of the poet, the one who has the *"making-power; it* [the poet's superiority] *is because he can create and they can only alter; it is because things grow in his mind from the seed, and theirs are only sand gardens where children stick up rootless flowers . . . because he is* ποιήτης *which is what we call poet."* Brooks pointed out that the literal meaning of "poet" is "the person who makes something," but more than that the poet is the hero and the model for others. To be that sort of person, everyone needed a "pattern man whom he can thoroughly admire and esteem," who makes others "his servants in a servitude that does them honor," and whose words and acts are worth copying "because they are truly noble and trustworthy and true." In the poet's making, egalitarianism vies with elitism: "All men may be, and ought to be, poets all the time"[72]—but clearly are not. Brooks pointed out that poetry is disciplined thinking and writing; it sees and expresses more than any other type of art or intellectual enterprise. The true poet writes not for publication but for himself alone, and in doing so he disciplines himself to perceive and consent to the "song of the Almighty sing[ing] itself within his brain." The secret verses he writes are an aesthetic exercises that "help him to establish his identity, to prove his right to old hopes and thoughts and fancies, to his whole past self." In the general worminess of growing up, Brooks declared, some young person may write "poetry by stealth and [be] ashamed of it," perhaps because it is salacious, "but if it came from the heart thank God who put it in your heart to write it."[73]

According to Brooks, we each have "a closet in our soul that is not often opened." Inside, all is still as death; it is a closet filled with desires, antipathies, hopes, and fears, "all huddled in with one another," never stirring. "We are," he writes, "chilled at the cold deadness of the place," a place of powers never used. But the "true poet is the forger of a new key, and true poetry is the grand moving again of all that dead machinery." The poet's power is the "creator-power of making a world of beauty in the soul," and when this silent enginery is set into motion, "the young man [*any* young man or woman] stands stronger, firmer, truer. . . . [He commands those] powers around him as Adam did the beasts of Paradise, and gives them names." "That right of naming," Brooks declared, "vests him with the right of governing them too." When the young man knows the names of his adversaries—in Brooks's case rejection and failure, among other things—he can call them forth to "minister of their comfort to his despairing weakness."[74]

The argument was unquestionably autobiographical. Self-knowledge, which comes through the naming of hopes, fears, and desires, keeps back the darkness, gives power to hate, and despises "all unhealthy dreams" to widen one's understanding of reality, to "reach outside of earthly things and live in daily sympathy with the beauty of spiritual natures." Brooks believed that as he learned "of the unity and harmony of our existence," he could feel himself "outgrowing our contempts" and self-condemnations, seeing each day as "high and pure and rich in worth and beauty."[75] He meant to be optimistic and liberating—and was, not only for himself in a time of personal despair, but for his generation, which was threatened with national despair. The noblest "poem" for him was that of the young man who, despite failure and conflict, went "unflinchingly about that duty [to God and humankind], fearing no taunt because it is up out of the reach of taunts as the stars are out of danger of the storms."[76] For Brooks, duty won out over despair through an act of the will. John Keble wrote: "Poetry is the indirect expression in words, most appropriately in metrical words, of some overpowering emotion, or ruling taste, or feeling, the direct indulgence whereof is somehow repressed."[77] Brooks saw duty as "poetry"—that of the sermon—which opened the locked door and set the machinery of emotion and feeling whirring.

What of Brooks's own poetry? It may be construed that he reserved for it his deepest feelings, especially, though by no means exclusively, his feelings of love. There has been a fair amount of speculation about Brooks's relationships with women. One of his biographers appears to want him to have had love affairs, however chaste, with certain women.[78] There was Jenny Fairfax, whom he met during his first year in theological school in Virginia. Her father "lived in great style, keeps a grand house, sets a splendid table and has one of the prettiest girls (age about eighteen years, one month, I should say) for a daughter that I ever saw." Clearly Brooks was smitten. "She is really quite stunning," he continued, "dark hair, and eyes, fine complexion, dresses tastily, lively, full of fun and cordial on first acquaintance."[79] During his second year in Virginia, he saw her frequently, at one point noting that "she is quite the belle this winter, and has cultivated ringlets during the summer which make her look prettier than ever."[80]

A romantic poem he wrote tells of lovers alone, away from the world, remote. From their "high window" they look upon the "street of human life." While inside their "happy home" is peace, without is "men's angry strife":

> Look out! see how strange eyes look here upon us,
> How poor they think our dwelling and how cheap;
> They dream not of our godlike joys and honors,
> The ripe, rich fields of blessing that we reap.

The hero bids his lover to "close the curtain!" lest peering eyes see their love, the "purest . . . and completest." They sit hand in hand, "nor dare to speak a word":

> So sit we by the soul's sweet fireside, fairest.
> The days go by as light winds kiss the flowers.
> They seek through all earth's sweetest and earth's rarest,
> A bloom so sweet, as love so rare as ours.[81]

Some months later, Brooks wrote bitterly of his and Jenny's separation:

> Ay, so you come again, I see.
> I wish you well but yet I know
> Though memory die and duty grow,
> Yet loving friends we cannot be.

He went on to speak of "distrust" and "discord" as the reason for their separation.[82] Was it personal? Was he referring to the growing discord between North and South and the angry debate that accompanied it? Or perhaps both? The last seems the most likely, but it is not provable.

Whenever Brooks was deeply moved, he wrote poetry. There is one case in which he wrote passionately of friendship with another male. Of meeting this particular friend after a long separation he said that he "trembled when to-day appeared":

> And so our greeting first was shy,
> But soon we answered love's demand.
> There came a warmth with meeting eye,
> And throbbing heart and grasping hand.

The poem was not in keeping with either his letters to friends or the other poetry of friendship that he wrote. He continued:

> We sat and talked. I saw how youth
> Had ripened to the perfect man,
> And how through all thy nature Truth
> Was working out her wondrous plan.[83]

Innocent enough, perhaps, for Victorian male friendships were often expressed with an intensity that would later, in the post-Freudian age, become suspect. At the time, however, the term "homosexual" was unknown, and the "language of ecstasy," to use Donald Yacavone's phrase, fit in well with the Coleridgean turn to heightened feeling, sentiment, and consciousness. "To a surprising degree," writes Yacavone, "mid-nineteenth-century social attitudes permitted great liberty in personal relations, largely untainted by homophobia."[84] As a result, the pleasures of male—and female—friendship were described vigorously and enthusiastically by the Victorians.[85] Moreover, in Christian circles the "idea of agape, or Christian love, underpinned the fraternal relations of antebellum reformers and abolitionists"—as well as of others—"just as it had been a dominant motif of the primitive Christian church." Agape began with the love of God the Father for the Son, and in its human form it "was rooted in Jesus' love for his disciples and their love for one another."[86] Among men, letters (and in this case poems) were often "effusive, affectionate, and intimate," revealing "an emotional intensity . . . similar to what feminist historians have discovered in the correspondence of nineteenth-century women."[87] While it is true that for the entire nineteenth century no consciousness of a homosexual person existed, it is also fair to say that sometimes there was a good deal more going on between the affectionate lines than authors realized at the time.[88]

In Brooks's case we simply cannot make a judgment. There are two or three intense poems about women; there is only one poem about a man that is the least bit "sexual." His letters to his male friends are not particularly effusive or full of affecting language. He was smitten by Tennyson's *In Memoriam,* but then who was not at the time? *In Memoriam* is a love poem expressing grief over the loss of a male "lover." However, the "piece cannot be understood," writes Yacavone, "unless placed within the context of nineteenth-century fraternalism and recognized as a masculine expression utterly at odds with traditional views of Victorian gender roles."[89]

What we do know is that Brooks was moved aesthetically by women as well as by men and that he maintained intimate friendships with both throughout his life. He spoke often of male purity and perfection and sought male heroes to serve as models for his age—ideal men who would bestow an optimism about human possibilities, one that stood in contrast to the increasing darkness that characterized the second half of nineteenth-century America. As Lewis Mumford observed in 1931, the "nation not merely worked differently after the Civil War: the country *looked* different—darker, sadder, soberer."[90] In the midst of both his own depression and the confusion of the 1850s, Brooks forged a satisfying ideal for daily life, not only for himself but for others.[91] He meant to be—and would become—the poet-preacher of that ideal in the great and beautiful temple built for him: Trinity Church, Boston.

That he paid a price in terms of limits on his personal life is evident. The despair Brooks experienced in 1856 reinforced a singleness of purpose in pursuit of the ideal he sought and eventually found. That ideal and also the "perfection" of his family's home life blocked out, as far as we know, consideration of the experience of erotic involvement with another. He claimed that if eros came in the front door of his mind he would welcome it and integrate it into the rest of his thoughts. But he apparently did not. We know he remained unmarried; whether his sexuality was repressed, released, or sublimated we cannot say. His age taught people "to postpone gratification, to repress themselves sexually, to improve themselves, to be sober, conscientious, even compulsive."[92] Mastery over one's "bad passions" was expected of all Christians and certainly of its leaders. The problem was that the two most powerful emotions, the religious and the sexual, each defied postponement and repression.

What is equally—perhaps more—important to understand is Brooks's artistry and accomplishment, forged by a sense of duty and sculpted by discipline and study. Both won him an audience. His manhood was simple, convincing, and shaped by an adversity that retained those hearers. His auditors also sensed that, in the midst of success itself, he remained essentially humble. Do you suppose a man "has never wrestled with his own success and happiness?" he asked. "'In all time of my prosperity, Good Lord, deliver me!'—'Deliver me!'—that is the cry of a man in danger, of a man with an antagonist. For years that man and his prosperity have been looking each other in the face and grappling one another."[93] The question for Brooks was whether the man should rule prosperity or it should rule him. Those who heard and knew Brooks were convinced that he was master of his antagonist.

During the summer of 1856, in the midst of intellectual and psychological perplexity, Brooks read Robert Browning's poem "Bishop Blougram's Apology." The piece had been published the previous year in a collection of poems called *Men and Women*. He was captivated by its style. He liked Browning's dramatic monologue and later used it in his preaching. In the sermon "Belief and Unbelief," he quoted Browning:

> Just when we're safest, there's a sunset-touch,
> A fancy from a flower—bell, someone's death,
> A chorus-ending from Euripides,—
> And that's enough for fifty hopes and fears,
> As old and new at once as nature's self.[94]

Just when Brooks himself thought he lived unthinking and apart from the poet's closeted power, in a world of particles, there came upon him the One. You could never be safe from the agents of communication, disturbing angelic messengers who set that unused machinery of the mind to work, enough for "fifty hopes and fears." In his sermon Brooks did not quote the rest of Browning's stanza, but he might well have for he knew it intimately. It told the story of his decision at the end of that summer:

To rap and knock and enter in our soul,
Take hands and dance there, a fantastic ring,
Round the ancient idol, on his base again,—
The grand Perhaps! We look on helplessly,
There the old misgivings, crooked questions are—
This good God,—what could he do, if he would
Would if he could—then must have done long since:
If so, when, where and how? Some way must be—
Once feel about, and soon or late you hit
Some sense, in which it might be, after all.
Why not "The Way, the Truth, the Life?"[95]

The decision came hard and even then contained a question, a perhaps. Brooks did not speak with his Episcopal rector, Alexander Vinton. Instead he went out to Cambridge to talk with James Walker, whom he venerated as a "confessor to souls."[96] Harvard's future president, Charles W. Eliot, then a tutor in chemistry, remembered seeing Brooks arrive at the president's office that day: his "face was of deathly whiteness, the evidence of some great crisis."[97] What transpired between Walker and his former student is unknown. A month later, however, Brooks quite suddenly left Boston for the Virginia Theological Seminary. The process from unfaith to at least assent, if not consent, that Browning had so aptly described in his poem proved to be the motor dynamic that sent Brooks on his first trip outside New England. In October 1856 such a journey was like going to a foreign country.

· · ·

Phillips Brooks had failed to measure up to the high standards set by his environment—a failure that wakened him from too-easy assumptions about himself. As a result, he determined to leave home, sort out his thinking apart from Boston and from an overpowering family, and make his own way. That he still relied heavily on his background—family, education, and social standing—soon became evident. While he supported the Evangelicals of Virginia in their theology, when he came up against their anti-intellectualism, the worst snobbery was brought out in him, which was understandable if not forgivable. The lonely youth from the cradle of revolutionary fervor found himself in the strange slave society of the South and he reacted with unattractive self-righteousness. More important, though, is the fact that amid the dissolution of the American nation, his quest for the ideal assumed great importance. Brooks learned from Shelley and others that there was an "indestructible order" and that poets were essential to the health and stability of societies because they alone "imagine and express" that order.[98]

4

Virginia Seminary: Slavery and Evangelicalism

The temptation to use the expression "wilderness experience" to describe Phillips Brooks's first year at the Episcopal Theological Seminary in Virginia should be resisted,[1] for there is nothing to indicate that he actually experienced wilderness life. Granted, the seminary lay in almost inaccessible woods, criss-crossed only by paths and overlooking the Potomac River. Brooks, who arrived two weeks late, drove a hired buggy from Alexandria "until the road seemed to end in a fence and forest" and very little else. He had in fact lost his way. "Tying his horse, he explored and found the Seminary in a grove."[2] What was more, he wrote to his brother William, "My lordly apartment is a garret in an old building called the Wilderness." The ceiling was too low and the bed was too short. "I looked in for a moment, threw down my carpet bag, and ran." Later he also confessed: "I am in a perfect wilderness of names, for they've been introducing me all around and I shan't know half of them again."[3]

"Culture shock" would better describe how Brooks felt upon his arrival in Virginia. To begin with, he told William, "Everything seems about half a century behind the age." The South was "a mean and wretched country at best, so far as I have seen it." He was also unprepared for his first encounter with slavery. The division between North and South, he wrote, "seems marked most plainly where the blessing ceases and the curse begins, where men cease to own themselves and begin to own each other. . . . [The slaves] in the seminary are let out by their masters for so much a year, paid of course to the master just as you'd pay for a horse hired." When he first saw a caravan of wagons manned by slaves coming from the interior of Virginia, he noted that the blacks seemed "jolly and happy," but then he quickly added, "which to my mind makes it [slavery] all the worse." Not only was slavery immoral, but, given his practical nature, Brooks also felt it was inefficient. It took forever, he declared, to get a job done, "and fifty forevers to get it done decently, even in the littlest things."[4] In December 1857, during his second year at the seminary, he noted that "just now they have patrols out to look for unruly slaves which, it seems, is an annual custom about Christmas time, a pleasant little way of keeping the festival."[5] He was also shocked at the return of fugitive slaves. Brooks wrote to his father: "The boy that used to make my bed last term has made tracks for the North during vacation & is advertised in the *Alexandria Gazette* with 150$ reward offered"—to which he added derisively, "If you should meet him any where at the north, there is a chance, you see, to make a little something by a Fugitive Slave speculation."[6]

Brooks himself was not free from racial prejudice, or at the very least human insensitivity. He laughingly told how he got an elderly slave to stand on his head while he—Brooks—placed two nickels on the edge of his desk. The black man did as he was bidden but then quickly righted himself, grabbed the money, and bolted off without a word. Brooks commented that the slave seemed ungrateful.[7] Still, Brooks proved loyal to the abolitionist's cause. He reported in other correspondence with his father that the *Atlantic,* with its "belligerent articles [against slavery,] reached here without being intercepted" and he thereupon "put it in the Reading Room with a good deal of curiosity as to what would come of it." Two days later it was missing. "I had the satisfaction of inquiring for it in public, but so far it has not been heard from." Shortly thereafter, some northern students who held a prayer meeting for the seminary's and the neigbhors' slaves were "informed that there was tar and feathers ready" if they went far from the grounds. "In general they [the students] have been given to understand that their tongues were tied and they were anything but free [to preach]. . . . A pretty style of life, isn't it?" Brooks asked his father.[8]

During his son's time in Virginia, William Brooks feared that Phillips was "not aware" of the importance of acting discretely in all matters between the North and the South, "remembering it is a delicate subject on both sides." The elder Brooks was concerned that "positive evil" might befall the young man and his friends despite—or perhaps because of—"the weakness of their [the South's] case."[9] During the years that followed, however, the antislavery convictions of the Brookses deepened. "I am sitting alone this evening," wrote Mary Brooks in late May 1859, "everybody has gone out somewhere, either to an anti-slavery meeting or somewhere else."[10] Five days later, William Sr., writing from Boston—that "cockpit of [the] new revolution"[11]—described his own conservative reactions to Massachusetts's compliance with the Fugitive Slave Act of 1850: "Your friends in the Anti-Slavery [Society] were much as usual, & our Cousin Wendell [Phillips] at times beside himself particularly when he said that the State proclamations should be changed & instead of 'God save the Commonwealth of Massachusetts,' it should be 'God damn the Commonwealth of Massachusetts.' Wasn't that outrageous?"[12]

On the eve of the Civil War, Phillips wrote a letter in Latin—hitherto untranslated—to his brother Frederick, partly to test the boy's budding classical ability, but also because he knew, by this time, to be careful in what he wrote and spoke. By the "Kalends" of February 1859, there was no mistaking the letter's tone of approaching crisis over the slavery issue. "Because war is about to occur, my dear Fred, when you most excellent man will be sent to the senate of our Republic, you will see clearly that things here in the South are very different from those we have always enjoyed in the North. This entire region seems blind in one eye and in the other is paralyzed by a great black stain, the name of which is slavery." It was just as well that the concluding paragraph was written in another tongue: "Thus to me this region seems in the grave of this great nation though for blacks which it fatefully oppressed, a worse death was in store—to be sacrificed, to be burned, and to be killed daily."[13] Whatever the haste of his Latin composition, there was no mistaking the passion—and the revulsion—of the writer. In 1862, as rector of Holy Trinity Church, Philadelphia, Brooks began a movement to desegregate the streetcars of the city. He preached frequently to black Union soldiers, joined the Freedmen's Relief Association, and announced "most solemnly for

Negro suffrage."[14] His experiences in Virginia contributed directly to his "radical" Republicanism.

. . .

With regard to the southern society that surrounded the Episcopal Theological Seminary and in which he moved freely, Brooks showed a patronizing attitude, not altogether pleasant, since he appears to have accepted hospitality freely. "'The Season' in Virginia is in full blast just now," he wrote in late November 1857. "I have been to one big party & two little ones; each only equalled in stupidity by the others."[15] He took offense when the "prettiest young lady in Fairfax Co.," in a tactless remark, congratulated him on his name, which he shared with Preston Brooks, the congressman from South Carolina who had recently used his cane to beat Massachusetts senator Charles Sumner senseless on the floor of the senate.[16]

At Christmastime, Brooks had a "sort of half invitation which I suppose could easily ripen into a whole one to spend the vacation at the gubernatorial mansion in Richmond, but my taste for the great southern fire-eater [Henry Wise, governor of Virginia] is not yet ready to stand such close propinquity."[17] He was chagrined to learn that a few months later his cousin Edward Everett was only too glad to join Governor Wise in Richmond and give an address on the anniversary of George Washington's birth.[18] Brooks's attitude cannot alone be explained by Boston Brahmin loftiness but must be accounted for in terms of the growing sectional hatred. Clearly, northerners such as Brooks "gave as good as they got in this warfare of barbs and insults."[19] Still, Brooks probably should have been more circumspect in expressing his opinions. He did not hide the fact that, as a Massachusetts Republican, he was "a strong Frémont man"[20]—even though, at the time, the "very existence of the Republican Party threatened the security of the South."[21] The strange surroundings, the intensity of the issues, and indeed the breaking up of the nation all served to increase what might be explained as normal defensiveness. Brooks was, after all, only twenty when he arrived in Virginia and fresh from a personal crisis.

About his fellow theological students from the South and in general, Brooks showed himself to be complacent and less than generous. He confided to a college friend, "They are insufferably ungenial, narrow, and disagreeable, but I take the liberty of seeing very little of them." He had to admit, however, that "there are one or two who are among the finest . . . I ever happened to meet"—to which he added snobbishly, "We make quite a collegy little circle by ourselves and [are] looked on by the Polloi as outcasts." Still, he liked his situation "quite well, work pretty hard, read considerably and live really quite a pleasant life."[22]

Brooks could not blame his unease on being surrounded by southerners, for he was not. During the seminary's first quarter century of its existence, the student body was equally divided between North and South, with a strong border state representation. Perhaps surprisingly, in the 1850s there was a decided shift in favor of northern students; in 1859, the year of Brooks's graduation, thirty of forty-seven students were northerners. The location of the seminary's graduates is also revealing. As early as 1849, of its 194 graduates, 80 had parishes in the North, 30 in border states, 8 overseas, and 76 in the South; from 1850 to 1857, the shift northward was evident: 47 of the graduates of those years had parishes in the North, 7 in the border states, 5 overseas, and only 17 in the South.[23]

If Brooks's snobbery and sense of being out of place were tempered with time, his scorn for the anti-intellectualism of the Evangelicals at the seminary and elsewhere was not. Twenty years later in the Lyman Beecher Lectures on Preaching, he remained unyielding. He recalled his first impression of worship and classroom at the Virginia seminary: "I had come from a college where men studied hard but said nothing about faith. I had never been at a prayer meeting in my life. The first place I was taken to at the seminary was the prayer meeting; and never shall I lose the impression of the devoutness with which those men prayed and exhorted one another. Their souls seemed exalted and their natures were on fire. I sat bewildered and ashamed, and went away depressed." On the next day he met the same men at Greek class: "It would be little to say of some of the devoutest of them that they had not learned their lessons. Their whole way showed that they had never learned their lessons; that they had not got hold of the first principles of hard, faithful, conscientious study. The boiler had no connection with the engine. The devotion did not touch the work which then and there was the work and the only work for them to do." He knew where the steam went: it was employed in a "sort of amateur, premature preaching [that] was much in vogue among us. . . .

A feeble twilight of the coming ministry we lived in." Even the people in the neighborhood churches were contemptuous "and dubbed us 'parsonettes'."[24] He firmly believed that "all mental carelessness lessens our capacity of faith, makes us not only less believing but less able to believe, destroys as far as it can our power to rest on testimony for truth."[25]

Then there was the whole question of vocation. Brooks was hardly enthusiastic when he wrote to "Top" Sawyer that he had "settled down into what I suppose is to be my life, theology."[26] Nor did the course of study at the seminary fire his interest. At first he was unable to get the books he craved. "This is such an out of the way place," he complained to his father in March 1857, "where one has to buy all the books he wants, very different from Boston or any city where you can get at the libraries and borrow books." The seminary's library, which contained a scant eight thousand volumes, "is really worth just nothing at all."[27] At a later date he added: "There's no use mincing it. Egregiously dull and stupid. I don't like, I confess, to recite to a man, even with the common Greek education of Cambridge but that not particularly well learned, I can catch tripping as I can Dr. Packard whom as a good man and as a good Christian I respect heartily but who as a scholar & professor has outlived his usefulness."[28]

No doubt Brooks was suffering as much from homesickness for his Greek classroom at Harvard as from the errors, if they were such, of his New Testament professor at Virginia. Joseph Packard was a fellow New Englander, a graduate of Phillips Academy, Bowdoin College, and Andover Theological Seminary. One would suspect that such links with Brooks's background and such excellence as those institutions required would have mitigated criticism as well as loneliness. Moreover, given the nearly complete attention to Latin and Greek grammatical construction to which Packard had been exposed in the 1820s—this was before the advent of historical, critical methods of exegesis—the kind of mistakes Brooks claimed his professor made seem doubtful. Packard had studied under the renowned Moses Stuart, who in turn had recommended him highly to the trustees of the Virginia seminary as "fit for any Faculty." More gracious about his pupil than his pupil was about him, Packard remarked that Brooks was "the only student I have ever known who took out of the library the Latin and Greek classics, and kept up those studies while here."[29]

Given his apparent disdain, it is a wonder that Brooks stayed at Virginia Theological Seminary at all. In truth, he meant not to. But where else could he go in 1856–57? Educational prospects in other Episcopal centers of theological education appeared equally dismal. He confessed that "New York [General Theological Seminary] from what I am learning is not far in advance of this." There was Andover, of course, which had been founded by his family and which he and his friend C. A. L. Richards considered: "It is the most full of life & is in reality the place from which almost all the theology of this seminary comes at second hand."[30] As a model for theological education, it certainly had no equal among Protestants.[31]

Throughout the spring, Brooks and his family exchanged letters and pondered his discontent. By June, he and another classmate, Henry C. Potter, had learned that Potter's father, Bishop Alonzo Potter of Pennsylvania, was about to begin a new, competitive seminary in Philadelphia, and Brooks wrote home: "I think from all that I hear, it is going to be much better than this."[32] Unfortunately, the new seminary was not to open for another four years. Nor did Brooks transfer to Andover. President Edwards Amasa Park was, it seems, not enthusiastic about having extra Episcopalians on his campus, no matter who they were.[33]

During his first year of theological education, Brooks went quickly through the required work, writing papers on the history of Israel, the books of Kings and Nehemiah, on Boniface (the eighth-century missionary to Germany), and two subjects that appear to have interested him in particular: the style of New Testament Greek and the third-century theologian Origen. In his free time, he discovered in the seminary's library the Migne *Patrologia Graeca* and the *Patrologia Latina* and began to read the church fathers on his own.

What becomes evident in Brooks's written work in his first year is that he came to the Christian writers from a decided classical background and outlook. Brooks was sympathetic both with Origen's study of the classics and with his biblical interest. "Led by religious reverence false," Brooks noted, Origen at one point took up gnostic allegorizing. Teaching later at Caesarea, his learning became "pure & sincere." For Brooks, Origen "was the scholar of his time, earnest, thorough & as Christian as a man could be found." "Curious eyes" dwelt on his more extravagant statements on Scripture, and Origen became the "father of heresies." Brooks preferred his "plain, literal meaning of every line of scripture."[34]

Brooks also began Hebrew, which he referred to as "a tough old tongue, as independent as these thirteen [sic] United States, so that no little previous knowledge of any other language helps me at all."[35] He learned it rapidly but appears to have developed no appreciation of its beauty. He spoke of its "intractability[, which had] turned the Jews' thoughts into unnatural channels." Even when a "smoother tongue to write in gave him [the Jew] leave to choose his own course, sheer force of habit still kept him in the old." Turning to the New Testament, the young classical scholar from Cambridge was equally disparaging: for the most part the "style of New Testament Greek is a conglomerate dialect, drawn not from Athens in the time of its power but from the Greek colonies of Alexander and his successors ... full of provincialisms." There were too many words "which in their time were colloquialisms & never had reached the dignity of writing." Luke and Paul wrote better Greek, he declared, but generally the language of Christian Scripture "had all the disadvantages of being a poor, decayed tongue at best, used by men whose habits & associations lay in a language as different from it as Moses was from Pericles."[36] As usual, it was not so much what Brooks said as the way in which he said it.

At the end of May 1857, Brooks declared that he would not be back following the summer vacation: "I shall pack my books & other things in boxes and leave them here so that they can be sent for."[37] Yet he did return, albeit reluctantly, in the fall. This time he found increasing intellectual encouragement and friendship from the theology professor and dean, William Sparrow, who had been unwell for much of Brooks's first year.[38] Sparrow, like Packard, was from Massachusetts. Schooled in Ireland, to which his Protestant and Evangelical family had returned for some years, he had graduated from Columbia University, become professor of Latin and Greek at Miami University, and moved on to the theological school of Kenyon College.[39] In the intervening time he was ordained in the Episcopal church and had taken up the study of theology and church history. Sparrow, a disciplined, clear-headed scholar with the ability to think abstractly, to hold his opinions and not be held by them, was also a mathematician.[40]

When Sparrow moved to the Virginia Theological Seminary in 1841, he brought Arminianism with him. His ideas were characteristic of that theology. Grace was defectible, insofar as it was subject to rejection by insouciant, ungrateful men and women. For Sparrow,

God *offered* salvation to humankind and then waited for a response. Faith was essentially "something to be laid hold of."[41] The rest of the professors at the seminary had been and, during Sparrow's tenure, remained Calvinists,[42] but Sparrow was not a liberal Daniel in the Genevan lion's den. While angry growls were heard elsewhere on the subject of free will, all was quiet in the Episcopal lair—at least on this subject. Evangelical Episcopalians were comfortable with the language of both election and free will.[43]

In addition, there were broad areas of agreement. Sparrow and his colleagues saw faith as reliance on the atoning sacrifice of Christ and as the sole means of attaining salvation. Together they believed that humankind was guilty and polluted, was in imminent danger of hell, that Christ restored perfect obedience to God for humans' sake, and that Christians lived by the sanctifying power of the Holy Spirit.[44] Further, Sparrow appears to have agreed wholeheartedly with the theological position of Bishop William Meade of Virginia, whose thought Sparrow outlined and commended. Meade disbelieved the doctrine of apostolic succession, refused to deny the validity of non-Episcopal orders, repudiated transubstantiation (as expected), and saw the chief function of the church as that of teaching the Bible, witnessing to Christ, and performing acts of mercy. In all of this the sacraments were a means to an end and "of great help to the believer."[45] These evangelical principles, Sparrow remarked elsewhere, "are the principles of the Bible, and of the Church, mother and daughter [England and America], and . . . have been the life-blood of the Missionary cause, both foreign and domestic."[46]

Such views became part of Brooks's theological culture. There were other aspects of Sparrow's attitude that the young man absorbed as the two talked in the teacher's study during many evenings. Sparrow had a distaste for churchmanship issues and for theological wrangling. He wanted the church to focus on the "conversion of sinners and the sanctification of saints," and he urged his students to "eschew all dogmatic questions, and ecclesiastical questions, and all other questions that might call attention from that one thing," the person of Christ.[47] Election, Sparrow asserted, is "not systematically discussed anywhere in Scripture, though it is by implication, taught everywhere." Still, his Evangelicalism never kept him from urging the importance of either hard work or rational discourse, so long as it was polite. In writing and preaching, Sparrow demanded that students "arrange it rightly, . . . bring it forth with true art, which of course, is art concealed . . . and [throughout] disciplining one's own mind."[48] The Boston Latin School had already done that for Brooks.

Increasingly in his second year, Brooks began to describe and define the ultimate, ideal hero whom he sought and whom, over a lifetime, he would describe in the light and imagery—and sometimes light-imagery—of Platonism and neo-Platonism: Jesus Christ. Brooks now moved beyond the heroes of his boyhood essay "Roman Examples of Devotion to Country,"[49] beyond Boswell's *Johnson,* Carlyle's impressionistic and panoramic *Cromwell,* the mad Shelley, and Goethe, that "soul sent by God."

But the path was not direct. Brooks became aware of a religious road he did not wish to travel. The theology textbook that Sparrow introduced into the Virginia seminary—and the one that was used, astonishingly enough, until 1898—was the two-volume *Lectures on Christian Theology* by George Christian Knapp, the early nineteenth-century German pietist and antischolastic Lutheran from Halle.[50] Andover's Leonard Woods had translated and introduced these volumes to the American scene, and their appearance in Virginia marked a change from earlier Calvinist fare to a type of study that, Woods exulted, "is happily turning more and more to the inward scroll of experience."[51] It was a fateful statement, one that was to prove astonishingly true—for good or ill—at the Virginia Theological Seminary for the next century and a half. Beginning with Knapp, pietism had now gotten its nose officially into the Calvinist tent pitched in the wilderness of northern Virginia by the Evangelical Episcopalians. The turn to inward experience, Woods judged, had come about under the influence of Schleiermacher, "one of the profoundest theologians in Germany."[52]

Knapp was another matter. However profound the thinking of Schleiermacher, that of Knapp was predictable, superficial, monotonous—and safe. It sent the student back to Scripture at every turn, not to plumb its depths, but to search the text in support of a particular reading of Lutheran doctrine. If the seeds of such a method were in Luther's own approach to Scripture—a debatable point[53]—there was a moralism to Knapp's thought that would have made the great reformer erupt in cheerful abomination. Fortunately, Brooks knew bad theology when he saw it. He wrote to Joseph Packard in 1886, "I have never looked at Knapp since [leaving the seminary]"; the book was, in his opinion, "very dull and dreary."[54]

The German from Halle wanted little more than to ensure better behavior. To achieve that worthy goal, however, he imprisoned the doctrine of justification by grace through faith behind preceptorial bars, thereby making any enjoyment of it by the believer virtually impossible. With something less than enthusiasm, Knapp had declared that forgiveness of sins was "one of the greatest benefits which no one can do without." He then went on to spoil what should have been a matter of great joy and comfort to all poor sinners by gloomily—and unbiblically—advising that "no one may be sure of his forgiveness." Knapp suggested to his pietistic—that is, true as opposed to nominal Christian—followers that assurance did not rest on feeling "but on actual compliance with the conditions of which God will forgive our sins." "If," he continued, "anyone finds in himself the signs of true faith, of sincere love to God in Christ, of a renewed heart, and of virtuous Christian disposition, he is justified." It was as if Jesus Christ had not done his work already in behalf of everyone. There was no mistaking Knapp's meaning: a person "may receive pardon at any time while life continues, *so soon* as he fulfills the requisite conditions of forgiveness." He wanted this "last clause . . . carefully and expressly annexed in order to preserve men from security and carelessness in sin." Conviction of sin and repentance then preceded the gift of faith for Knapp, while justification followed, if not on good works, then on something close to them. Free grace was gone. To those who might come to the "actual enjoyment of the promised forgiveness," the Halle theologian reminded them that they were "under indispensable obligation to live henceforth in the strictest obedience to the divine commands from grateful love to God and to Christ."[55] Knapp failed to see the irony in his statement: that the response of "grateful love" to Christ on the part of men and women might come before and render unnecessary Knapp's own graceless reminder of "indispensable obligations." As it was, behavior motivated by gratitude seemed almost an afterthought.

Despite the dreariness of these theological tomes, Brooks observed, they "served as a glass" in which Sparrow, a spirited professor of theology, might shine by comparison.[56] One wonders if the price, for the students at least, was not a bit high. Brooks's own thought, aesthetic rather than moralistic, emerged slowly in papers on the Anglican church's Articles of Religion and, later in his second year, in one on Christology.

In his essay on the Thirty-nine Articles, it is clear that Brooks was not so much interested in fastidious obedience to the letter of the moral code as in the biblical principles involved in the doctrine. First, he found certain truths underlying all of the Articles. They were "the sufficiency of Scripture, the Old Testament not destitute of Christ, man's fallen nature, God's grace alone redeeming mortal will, the insufficiency of dead works and the absurdity of works of supererogation." Second, he boldly declared that all of the doctrines in the Articles "lead or are led directly to the central doctrine of justification by faith in the Lord Jesus. All either speak out of it as a necessary part of a universal plan of salvation or else we see directly the way in which it [justification] follows upon them as the only way of answering the need that they unfold. All truth becomes one truth in Jesus."[57] The content of the final sentence was to become the focus of Brooks's theology for the rest of his life. Of the primacy of free grace, offered by Christ, one could have joyful assurance without conditions. And that grace, with its frequent justification of the humble believer, was to be seen preeminently in the cross at Calvary. Brooks wrote that in the cross we see the "awful grandeur of divinity in the spirit that came and bore that agony, as well as in the earth that quaked & the tombs that were rent & the graves that were opened when Jesus died."[58] The Article on justification preserved the meaning of the cross and for that reason, in Brooks's estimation, dominated all other Articles. Of necessity the others related to it.

For Brooks every Article of the thirty-nine "has its negative as well as its positive side." On the negative side, he wrote, "there is a central error and cluster around it." Justification by the works of the law, rejected by Paul, "is the error on which all the others hinge." Brooks saw that "starting from that [error] we are ready to deny the sufficiency of Scripture . . . ; we have made our old Bible useless, disowning all its scheme & made a new one either in tradition or elsewhere." Thus the grace of the Gospel would be banished from the Old Testament, disowned in the New, and rendered blind to the great and merciful act of Calvary. "We are ready to turn [to] Pelagius at once for without the doctrine of grace by Christ, the doctrine of sin by Adam deserving wrath and punishment is monstrous as Pelagius said it was." Once the Pelagian route was chosen, two desperate alternatives presented themselves, "either to deceive ourselves & say we have no sin or making conscience judge with no advocate to speak for us."[59]

The second alternative seemed to Brooks almost worse than the first, for in it we "stand convicted to ourselves of unpardonable transgression." The principle of justification by works—or *germ,* as he preferred to call it—thereafter ripened and unfolded, so that the "whole soul is a holocaust to error & every step forward is of necessity a step wrong, every progress is to perdition, every development a [preparation?] for death." His conclusion was that the "fundamental deceit" of self-justification—that is, of unfaith in Christ the gracegiver—led willy-nilly to damnation. We bring this "resurrection to damnation" on ourselves, Brooks declared. "Do we not see just what Jesus meant, when, after dwelling on God's love & willingness to save, he said, 'He that believeth not *is* condemned *already,* because he hath not believed in the only begotten son of God . . . already in rejecting one truth he has rejected all those truths which not only bring life [but] which *are* life & peace & joy in the Holy Ghost."[60]

There is in humankind, Brooks reminded us, a "willful blindness that calls itself a search light, this crying out that Jesus does not answer our profane demands . . . at every irreverent call of ours." And it was the idea of rejection of the grace and blessing of the cross that led Brooks in his notebook to imaginatively reconstruct the rest of the day of the Crucifixion when "Calvary is deserted & the cross is taken down & the midday darkness has grown bright again, then strange misgivings shall grow strong." Life returns to the ordinary. Doubt begins to seep in. The glory fades. We do not *want* to believe. "Pharisee-like we would build a sepulchre to the prophets that our fathers slew," Brooks wrote, adding in grim terms: "To all such vain self-righteousness comes the warning, 'Ye shall seek me but ye shall not find me. Whither I go ye cannot come.'" For Brooks there was no claiming of salvation, "not till we recognize ourself in all that Calvary scene, not till we see our nature in all that hate."[61]

• • •

Placed in the context of the crisis in his own life, in that of the institution of the church, and in that of the nation itself in the late 1850s, Brooks's words take on an added poignancy. It is not at all improbable that each of these crises contributed to his fixing on the centrality of the cross.

With respect to Jesus' act of justification of humankind at Calvary, once it was accepted, then according to Brooks "man owns all truth & so from its being planted in him all perfections spring up in him till he stands before God in the perfectness of Christ." Elsewhere he concluded, "God is glorified in justifying man & man is justified in glorifying God."[62] As he could correct the Greek of his New Testament professor, so he could improve on the theological textbook he was required to read. And as he did so, his thinking moved inevitably from justification to sanctification, from Christ's one act of reconciliation to his continuing influence on the lives of those who trusted him, from covenant to eschatology and ethics.

5

The Search for the Ideal: Reading the Text for Oneself

In terms of his formal evangelical theology, in his attitude toward Anglican claims to apostolic succession, and in his reluctance to join liturgical and ecclesiological debates, Phillips Brooks was influenced by William Sparrow. He was not, however, a carbon copy of his favorite professor at the Episcopal Theological Seminary in Virginia. Though we have no record of the frequent conversations between the two, Brooks was part of another generation. His wide reading in the Romantics and his natural independence of mind led him along a different path from that followed by Sparrow. Specifically, in what came to be the most important doctrine for Brooks—that of sanctification, or the Christian life—he struck out on his own. In working out the philosophy that informed morality and aesthetics—"moral philosophy," as it was usually called, though sometimes "moral science"—the two men diverged. When placed beside the philosophical house in which Sparrow resided, the frame and substance of Brooks's abode is more sharply variant.

Sparrow was a realist in the tradition of Bishop Joseph Butler, the Earl of Shaftesbury, Francis Bacon, Richard Hooker, and, of course, Thomas Aquinas and ultimately Aristotle himself. As did many of his generation, Sparrow inherited the ideas of Scottish Common Sense philosophy.[1] Early on in his career he read the works of his immensely influential American contemporary Francis Wayland, a Baptist minister, reformer, moralist, and president of Brown University. Wayland and the Scottish Common Sense tradition provided a comforting and comfortable reaction to the skepticism and mechanistic psychology let loose in the eighteenth century by David Hume and David Hartley respectively. To counteract skepticism as well as religious emotionalism, Wayland and others found simple patterns—laws in nature and rules in human conduct—that were independent of and anterior to experience. Wayland was comforting when in 1835 he declared that "moral obligation is a peculiar and instinctive impulse, arising at once by the principles of our constitution, as soon as the relations are perceived in which we stand to the beings, created and uncreated, with whom we are connected."[2] Sense perception, or experience, made good on the principles. But more important, no longer did those who yearned for moderation and reasonableness have to put up with Jonathan Edwards's daring, frightening metaphysical supernaturalism. Edwards's assertion that God was the *immediate* cause and not just the first cause of all that was in nature and in human psychology sounded to many both arbitrary and dangerous. One could not sustain such belief, they felt, in the workaday world. By positing a moral faculty in human beings, Common Sense ethicists no longer had to cope with a potentially eruptive, sovereign God.

But the price was high: the monkey of good behavior was now on their backs. "That we do actually observe a moral quality in the actions of men, must, I think, be admitted," Wayland judged. He claimed that every human was conscious of this *"distinct and separate quality"* from childhood and that "all that is necessary to the prosecution of the science, is that it be admitted." Granting men and women the compliment of a natural moral faculty was comfortable, superficially at least, because it enhanced human powers of perception. An "intelligent and universal First Cause" made all things "capable of affecting us, both as individuals and as societies," he wrote. Then he went to the heart of the issue: "we are capable of observing these relations and of knowing how various actions affect us and affect others." Wayland believed that by "the light of nature we discover moral truth which could never be discovered by conscience unassisted." Thus, as he put it, "natural religion *presents additional motives* to the practice of virtue." He then qualified the gift of merit presented to humankind in the Bible (particularly the New Testament) by declaring that Jesus Christ was made "*available* to us on no other conditions than those of supreme, strenuous, and universal moral effort after perfect purity of thought, and word and action."[3]

Sparrow had used Wayland's *Elements of Moral Science* when he taught at Kenyon College. But he also had taken the work of Butler, William Paley, and Wayland and created manuscript lectures called "Questions and Notes," which he not only shared with those teaching in the mission field but which he "re-cast at about the time when he removed to Alexandria; reduced in amount, and expressed with more terseness." That in the revised form of his theology and moral philosophy Sparrow omitted "extracts and references to current literature" may account for the silence regarding the teaching of Wayland's *Elements* at the Virginia seminary.[4] Nonetheless, as far as Sparrow was concerned, Wayland fitted in nicely with George Christian Knapp. What is more, it was all quite "scientific" and could be buttressed by Paley's lockstep, mechanical view of revelation in his *Evidences of Christianity* and with Butler's intuitive principles of morality, together with his limits on reason, in *Analogy of Religion*. Since Sparrow was a mathematician as well as a theologian, neatness was appreciated. Defensiveness against skepticism was also the order of the day.

Not all of what Sparrow had to say was new to Brooks. President James Walker, to whom he had gone for advice in the summer of 1856, followed the Common Sense tradition and had himself abridged Dugald Stewart's three-volume *Philosophy of the Human Mind*. What is more, during Brooks's undergraduate years, Harvard's philosophy department was uniformly realist. Still, the winds of change—toward idealism—had begun to shift the philosophical basis of theology as the two disciplines moved along pretty much in tandem at mid-century.[5] Brooks's wide reading in the classics, the English and German Romantics, and the church fathers gave him a grounding in Platonic, middle Platonic, and neo-Platonic thought. Thus he came to look not toward God understood as First Cause but as the Ideal One. His moral philosophy led him to seek the absolute good rather than to strive to find in humans an intuitive moral faculty.[6]

Brooks searched for that absolute good in his heroes, in certain characteristics of his Puritan ancestors, and finally and preeminently in the person of Jesus Christ. As the subject of academic concern, moral philosophy per se ceased to interest him. Gone was any concern for natural religion as a force to move the human spirit. The attempt to make moral and psychological insights "scientific" gave way before the greater comprehensiveness and "grasp" of poetry itself. In theological terms, sanctification and the Christian life was henceforth, for Brooks, to be linked to Christ, the poetic inspirer of preachers and parishioners alike. More technically, the formal cause of justification was the imputation to us of Christ's righteousness for the forgiveness of our sins. But that imputation was best seen through the eye of the Coleridgean poet who made the doctrine "come alive." Sanctification must also be linked to Christ and, imperfect though it was in this life, was also by grace through faith. Here too Brooks sought to make that life aesthetically attractive for his hearers. It had dimensions of beauty that apparently Knapp, Wayland, and Sparrow did not understand. Henceforth, for Brooks, theology was to be on the offensive, not the defensive.

In Brooks's view, conversion to the faith and the subsequent Christian life were not one-time experiences. The commitment constantly had to be renewed. At the same time there was a continuing tension in the Christian's life between appreciation of God's reconciliation in Christ and awareness of the confusion and evanescence of existence. Sounding very much like Tennyson, Brooks expressed his innermost thoughts in poetry:

> We cannot keep the grace we win;
> We lost the heaven we thought we found;
> The same old world of strife and sin
> Girds all our meagre being round.
>
> Yet it was well to step awhile
> Across the threshold of our life,
> And see how God's more gracious smile
> Weds thought to faith as man to wife.[7]

If the poem's tentativeness about the perseverance of the converted saint hardly matches the fifth point of the Synod of Dort, there is nonetheless a degree of assurance marked, to be sure, by the back-and-forth struggle between divine grace and life in the world of "strife and sin." Pride in what might be "achieved" in sanctification was hardly an option. Inherent righteousness in sanctification was tentative but ever a possibility and a hope—by the grace of God.[8] The preacher's task was to awaken that hope, to show its inherent beauty, to stimulate the desire, not just of the feelings but of the understanding as well, so that the superior power of the Christ figure would take hold of people's lives. Brooks would do this by wedding aesthetics and morals; and he was confident that those who heard would in gratitude emulate Christ in his life and teaching.

Sanctification, then, meant movement toward the figure and pattern of Christ, his "perfect manhood." Giving adequate expression to that figure consumed Brooks's energies during his years as a theological student. Christ was the embodied truth of God's divinity. In Platonic fashion, Brooks engaged in a dialectic between the particular (Jesus) and its universal reality (that God was in Christ). Everything he read in nineteenth-century poetry, in the church fathers, and even in the Greek and Latin classics had to contribute to this central theme in his mind which he sought to express or else be cast aside. Above all, the four Gospels of the New Testament received careful literary and aesthetic analysis. Dispensing for the most part with commentaries, Brooks went directly to the original sources, treating them as works of art to be appreciated firsthand.

Throughout his three years of theological school, Brooks sought to give fresh and powerful expression to the center of his faith. In a remarkably mature sermon for a twenty-three-year-old, which he preached in the seminary's chapel in October 1858, his opening, autobiographical sentence reveals the direction and the intensity of his spiritual development: "How when we once get within the sphere of a great truth, we find all mental life seeking its center in it—thought, fancy, energy and faith, hope, fear, and speculation, all hurrying to the forum where their business is to be done and their fate decided." Thought, affection, and will converge in "the concentration of the moral life in Christ." God has set up this "grand Christ-truth, . . . a single fountain"; or, in a different metaphor, a single "door stands open to connect the two [God's world and ours]: I am the Way, the Truth, the Life."[9] Elsewhere Brooks spoke of the "subtle connection of the beautiful with the Good, making Jesus the true prophet of the Beautiful & opening the whole secret of Christian art."[10] For the next thirty-five years, until his death in 1893, he built onto this center of his thought.

Another, more mundane historical concern was Brooks's own Puritan heritage. He sought to discover what it might add to sanctification. History, it seemed, had some value for the Christian life, and so he wrote a paper on Puritanism. It was a very carefully written essay, maybe a first and personal draft, but neat, dated 3 November 1857, possibly done for his course in English and American church history which came that year. Whatever the occasion, he was picking up from where he left off with Carlyle's *Cromwell*. The point is not so much the accuracy or inaccuracy of his reading of English Puritan history during the Civil War period as his attraction to the subject and his claim of continuity for that tradition with his own time and culture.

Brooks tried to describe for his own satisfaction the Puritan character. He knew it was complex; still, he said, we may try to understand the whole by looking to one element: "It was concise." Where the royalist was poor, the Puritan was rich in this quality. "It was this centralization which made the conciseness of his [the Puritan's] life, which grouped all the powers & properties that were in him into one series of thoughts and acts so consistent that they look down this perspective of 200 [years] like one single act and thought." Not very subtly, Brooks saw the Cavaliers as lacking in willpower and constancy: King Charles reluctantly and "sulkily" opened the Long Parliament. By contrast, consider a bold follower of Cromwell: "If he went to his Family, he was a Puritan there, training young Puritans for the Battles of the Lord. If he rode across the fallow field & up the rought hill at Naseby, stunning the frightened royalists with his battle cry, 'God our strength,' he was a Puritan there doing a Puritan's not a soldier's work." Here, for the young Romantic, in the Roundhead's "compactness and completeness," was the secret of his power. But, Brooks asked ingenuously, "Was it then a secret?" Hardly. One need not go to Puritan or any history to find it, he declared. Observe New England itself, "for there this lesson is written."[11]

There was, according to Brooks, another side to the Puritans' singleness of purpose—that moment when revolutionary fervor bars compassion and irony from the court of public opinion and in so doing forgets the Gospel. If, he wrote, the English revolutionary who

stood in front of Whitehall Palace & saw his King die, saw the masked murderer holding the dead face & shout, "This is the traitor's head," when in the strangely powerful words of the old Historian, "A great shudder ran through the crowd that saw the dead then a shriek & then they all dispersed." There too he was a Puritan & went home and took down his Bible & read in ye spirit of a

Puritan law & not a Christian gospel, "So let all thine enemies perish, O Lord, but let them that love Thee be as the sun when he goeth forth in his might."

Thus unity of purpose was twisted by self-righteousness, self-righteousness by violence, and, last of all, unbelief came on "& then it fell." There was no doubt in Brooks's mind: "Error, Ignorance & Prejudice were there already; Pride came & the fatal conspiracy was full & then the good gave way."[12] The insight was worth passing on, for in it Brooks was engaging in that most Puritan occupation: self-criticism. He did so through a review of the movement he thought he understood best, and in so doing he gave expression to the "redemptive power of remorse and regret," which in that tradition, he determined, was a source of strength.[13]

However, it was the centrality of Scripture, "with which the Puritan was so familiar, from which he drew the types and patterns, and the forms from which his ideas were always shaping themselves,"[14] that proved to be even more important to Brooks's thought; it would also be what he spoke about at the end of his life. He only half recognized that the Puritans' location vis-à-vis the real world and its shape was narrated in the Bible, that Puritans were "included in that total narration and by means of it in the world it rendered faithfully."[15] They knew themselves to be easily and naturally included in that total narration—which was something Brooks and his age did not know about themselves. In the first place, seventeenth-century American Puritans had an overriding sense of a creation redeemed and perfected by a sovereign God. For their part, Brooks and his nineteenth-century contemporaries sought the transcendent perspective their ancestors had assumed. The grandsons and granddaughters had to appeal to a yet-to-be-realized ideal that they found in Jesus Christ, who alone was the providence and benevolence of God. In him was the ideal of personhood, the "place" of the interaction of human activity and divine will. To bring others to that place involved an appeal to conscience and to a sense of duty.

The second difference with the earlier Puritans was that for the nineteenth-century reconstructionist the biblical world had to be re-created. Seventeenth-century Puritan preachers (and nineteenth-century black slave preachers) had only to remind their listeners of that inexhaustible store of good counsel and open-ended possibilities in

Scripture to bring their congregations into the presence of Moses or Elijah or Jesus. Brooks had to analyze and take apart the world of his congregation and to rebuild it in that of the Bible. John Winthrop, John Cotton, and John Eliot had viewed their Bible as a flexible historical almanac; Brooks viewed it as a source of expressive imagery rather than historic precedent. As M. H. Abrams observed, the "year 1800 is a good round number . . . by which to signalize the displacement of the mimetic and pragmatic by the expressive view of art."[16] Brooks and his Romantic contemporaries in the pulpit and elsewhere had to become the lamps that projected light onto the less-available and increasingly strange biblical scene. In the beam of light they cast, others might see the ideal to which they pointed. Everything depended, however, on the preacher's ability to arouse attention and excite feeling in others. That in turn depended on how they themselves interacted with the object of their faith. The line of march from the Platonizing Puritans and the Cambridge Platonists (really Plotinists), such as Nathanael Culverwel to Wordsworth and Coleridge[17] and then to Brooks is clear. The congregation, for its part, watched—listened to—the interaction between the preacher's mind and his subject. As Brooks held up the ideal for them, they in turn asked, Is he—and it—genuine? His simplicity, literary skill, and obvious sincerity led his auditors to answer in the affirmative.

Of course, Brooks interpreted Puritan faith and life in terms of the expressiveness of his day. In an address to the New England Society of New York in 1892, he attributed to his Puritan ancestor John Cotton "the everlasting presence of the *ideal* in the lives of men."[18] Like others of his day he was making a conscious effort to relate himself to the Puritan tradition in America. In the process, he reflected George Bancroft's association of Puritanism with popular sovereignty, declaring that the "watchwords of the people" of New England had been—and, he suggested, still were—religious liberty, popular government, popular education, and the trusteeship of "the land and country in which [the] nation lives."[19] Not a wholly inaccurate statement, it combined reinvention with quite real legacies of at least general continuity in the reformed tradition.[20] "What the world needs today," he concluded, "is more Puritanism, not less Puritanism."[21] A few years earlier, however, he had expressed some doubt when he wrote to his brother Arthur that the celebration of Christmas and the Puritan forefathers "interfered with one another now just as much as they ever did." He even suggested that the Pilgrims "landed just before Christmas on purpose" so that the celebration of their landing "might forever interfere with the preparation of Christmas trees and Christmas sermons." On "Forefathers Day" he expostulated, "How glad I am they lived and that they don't live now!"[22]

Brooks's recognition of the differences, even to the symbolic one of Christmas, leads to the larger question of whether the various forms of cultural Puritanism retained some historical continuity with their predecessor. Did it come to an end after 1684, as Charles L. Cohen maintains?[23] Was it then followed by the altogether different pietistic, evangelical world of George Whitefield and Edwards? Did Hawthorne's or Bancroft's or anyone else's reinvention have any substantive connection with what went before? Did each reinvention reflect aspects of the past as well as contemporary prejudices?

In what way was Brooks related to the Puritanism of which he himself spoke and which comprised his roots? Lawrence Buell maintains that the new cultural formulation undertaken by the "historical fictionalizers" rewrote New England's past for different contemporary reasons: to guarantee the authenticity of the new nationalism (as in the case of Bancroft); to show Puritanism's "romantic otherness" from the nineteenth century; or to show Puritanism's continuousness with daily life. For Buell, the latter two approaches are characterized preeminently by Hawthorne, on the one hand, and Harriet Beecher Stowe, on the other. For Stowe, the Puritan tradition was not strange and dreamlike, as it was for Hawthorne, but was reality itself. Because she dealt with the chronologically closer Edwardsean revolution, the "felt vitality" of Puritanism appeared greater for her than for Hawthorne, who in *The Scarlet Letter* "identifies Puritanism chiefly with the doctrines and polity of the founders of the Massachusetts Bay Colony and the early settlements."[24]

At different times Brooks seems to have reflected each of Buell's three types of reconstruction and also added one of his own.[25] More connected with the English past than either Stowe or Hawthorne, Brooks was ambivalent about the Cromwellian period. He had a sense of recognition and felt the tug of attraction to the Puritan cause in the English Civil War, but he also recognized that unity of purpose could breed pride and self-righteousness. At the same time, like Bancroft, he associated American Puritanism with popular sovereignty. He also felt its otherness—and not necessarily romantically, as Hawthorne did; rather, he was glad the founding fathers were not around to spoil Christmas any longer. But ultimately he, like Stowe, could not get away from the heritage of his ancestors.[26] In addition, he participated in what Jan C. Dawson has called "the politicization of the Puritan tradition in mid-nineteenth-century America." During his education in the 1850s and his first pastorate in Philadelphia until the end of the Civil War, Brooks joined those antislavery northerners whose "absolutist conscience derived from the reconstruction of the Puritan tradition."[27]

After the slaves were freed, Brooks's conscience was no longer troubled. He failed to see that the postwar economic condition of both immigrants and former slaves was itself a form of slavery. Aside from the general sense in the North that the problem of slavery had been "solved"—resulting in what Robert Penn Warren called the "treasury of righteousness"—Brooks himself began to travel along a different road, one that had nothing to do with the politicization of the tradition. Now, in the late 1850s, he became more and more interested in the aesthetic. It was a not unnatural development considering his literary education.

. . .

In his last two years at Virginia Theological Seminary, Brooks moved beyond both Knapp and Puritan history. More and more in his notebooks one sees the highly motivated student recording for future preaching what excited him in his reading and studies. He wanted to become the poet-preacher. From Coleridge he had learned that the poet alone was able to give the listener a multidimensional, stereoscopic—and, it was thought, truer—perspective on the object being viewed. When he stated in one of his most famous sermons, "The Candle of the Lord," that "only a person can truly utter a person,"[28] what he meant was that only a poet possessed of a wide enough lens to describe the other, only the "poetry" of Jesus Christ's perfect personhood, can utter the divinity of God. And Jesus required poets among his followers to utter him. The preacher's task was a high, demanding calling that required the exercise of much unused machinery in the closet of the mind.

Only by such means could the promises of the Gospel be brought to the believer. In Brooks's case those promises were sung in the lyric cadences of nineteenth-century Romanticism. They made of Christ, as we have seen, the ultimate hero to whom the preacher appealed by means of analogies drawn primarily from nature or from contemporary, everyday life but not wholly excluding typological (Old Testament) figures anticipating Christ.[29] Such preaching involved the preacher's imagination and the piling on of a great deal of nonbiblical detail. As a result, the style may seem to us verbose. In the hands of a master like Brooks, however, the "poetry" always fitted the subject. But the result was that the sermons, at least when read, often lack the crispness and even the "modernity" of those of, say, Thomas Hooker.[30]

After his initial year of seminary, Brooks concurrently traveled a theological path alongside his ongoing literary one. It too was followed largely independently of his formal course work. Since his prior education had been in the classics rather than in philosophical analysis, the Greek and Latin theologians of the early church provided the basis of his theological education. It was a natural progression. The church fathers became his daily fare. As a result, he gave only cursory attention to Richard Hooker and to Butler and none at all beyond the Articles of Religion to the reformers of the sixteenth century, Martin Luther and John Calvin.[31] Had he tackled the corpus of Luther's works or, even more, Calvin's *Institutes of the Christian Religion*, there would have surely been a closer attention on Brooks's part to the texts of Scripture and less to Platonic and neo-Platonic images of light and so forth. And that attention in turn would have integrated the New Testament more clearly with reformed theology and its application to his own time. His exact contemporary Martin Kähler, like Brooks, was motivated by the doctrine of justification by grace through faith and had dared to organize and unfold an entire evangelical dogmatics around such a center.[32] Moreover, Kähler's "Science of Christian Doctrine," first published in 1883, would have been available to Brooks, who kept abreast of theological culture.[33] There were others in Germany, Scotland, and England who were Brooks's contemporaries, and surely he knew of them: Bishop Handley Moule, A. B. Bruce, Marcus Dods, and the slightly younger scholars Adolph Schlatter and P. T. Forsyth—none of them anticultural evangelicals. All were profoundly influenced by the Protestant Reformation.[34] Yet Brooks, as we have seen, was shaped as much by the nineteenth-century high literary culture of England—and Germany—for which Boston's elite had such regard.[35]

As earlier with Shelley's passion, so during his seminary years Brooks was struck by and responded to Tertullian's tartness and verve. There was in the writings of that ancient North African literary figure a knowledge of classical religion and philosophy that could not fail to appeal to Brooks. By attacking the pagan gods and their skeptical Roman worshipers, Tertullian beckoned Brooks along a clear path that led to the Christ of the *De Carne Christi*. It is not too much to say that this most "puritan" of the Latin fathers became a crucial figure in the young American's theological education. Brooks wrote in his journal: "There is meaning in Tertullian's question when [in chapter 15 of the *Apology*], having shown how the worship of Olympus and its gods, priests and people had alike become infidel and false, he asks, . . . [since] you despise the old falsehood, what can you do now but come and learn & reverence the truth?" Tertullian, he continued, "puts before us the dreariness of Roman skepticism and all skepticism since." "Bow then to our Christ," came the command. Brooks saw Tertullian "pointing to man's need to worship something, man's sense of human dependence that is the great proof that there is a God."[36] It was perhaps Tertullian through the eyes of Schleiermacher.[37]

There were other figures who bridged for Brooks the two worlds of ancient Rome, the classical and the Christian, the one he had learned in school and college and the other he was pursuing in the late 1850s. Among them were Clement of Alexandria, Origen—particularly his commentaries on Leviticus—Saint Augustine's strongly neo-Platonic *De Vera Religione,* and Boethius's suggestive—for Christians—*De Consultatione Philosophiae.* In an essay on Origen, Brooks noted both that theologian's study of the classics and his great biblical interest wherein "from the plain, literal meaning of every line of scripture, he passed to the extravagant imagery that has made his writing famous."[38] According to Alexander V. G. Allen, Philo of Alexandria, over whom Brooks "bent in more rapt contemplation than over any other ancient writer,"[39] provided the New Englander with the *logos* as supreme idea, the first-born of God, and the highest mediator between God and the world. No doubt Philo's combination of Platonism and Stoicism fitted well Brooks's mind as much as that philosopher's harmonizing of Greek culture and Jewish faith.[40]

At last Brooks came to the Gospels themselves, and he did so with a sense of wonder and even strangeness. While his view of Christianity's central figure came to maturity some fifteen years after he had

left theological school, both the content and the method of his thinking were already present in his mind. In the aforementioned sermon
preached before the seminary community in October 1858, entitled
"The Centralizing Power of the Gospel," and in his seminary notebooks, the seeds of Brooks's Bohlen Lectures at Philadelphia, "The
Influence of Jesus," were planted.[41]

This is not to say that Brooks was uninterested in the ongoing nineteenth-century examination of biblical texts. Throughout his life he
kept abreast of historical-critical matters, and, after immersing himself in the older biblical theology of Heinrich Ewald, he read Julius
Wellhausen, Karl Theodor Keim, Emil Shuerer, and others—all in the
original German.[42] But he never spoke publicly of these authors or
their works. They paled before the "personal Christ" of whom he
preached.[43] He believed in firsthand encounter with the texts and
through them had evolved an authentic answerability to them. He was
largely immune to what George Steiner has called the "Byzantine
dominion of secondary and parasitic discourse over immediacy, . . . of
the critical over the creative."[44] Nor did Brooks seek the immunities
of indirection. Instead, he plunged into the text itself. He was primarily interested in the intention and integrity of the Bible. Mandarin
commentators who domesticated Scripture instead of following its own
inner logic "secularize[d] the mystery and summons of creation."[45]
Brooks agreed wholeheartedly when he commented, "Looking away
from that central truth of Christ, there is no profaner work than Bible study."[46]

Brooks went further still in his argument. Apart from Jesus Christ,
he felt, there is only that atheism that substitutes the "frivolity of
culture or the pedantry of ethics for this divinity of truth." By contrast, for those who have "looked the gospel in the face . . . theories
and schemes and ceremonies grow tame and dead." Such is the
"Christian radicalism which, through the myriad shows and sem-
blances of human life, goes down directly to the heart of things." At
the heart, of course, was Jesus Christ and his "simplicity," which was
always in danger of fragmentation in an unsteady world. Brooks
called not for the "scientific" examination of the sources of the Judeo-
Christian tradition but, on the basis of the "great agony of Calvary,"
for a renewal of fellow-feeling, the "working out of the world's redemption."[47] Theology was not for him a "philosophical enterprise
resting on a set of statable, general criteria," as one analyst has put

it; rather, it was the property of the church and, as such, "a critical or normed self-description."[48] For Brooks, theology began with Scripture, focused on Christ alone (justification), and issued in kind-heartedness and charity (sanctification). "This new Christian simplicity," he told those gathered for the 1858 sermon at the seminary, "is not perfect till it recognizes the world's hope in its own." One becomes a participant with Christ in the world's redemption when one "begins to identify himself with the race," when one "multiplies his life eight hundred millionfold," when the "history of the race becomes his experience, the happiness of the race his glory, the progress of the race his hope." On that October evening in the seminary chapel he seemed to warn professors and students alike when he declared: "Let us be sure no Church is soundly conservative or positively and steadily advancing, that no philosophy is wise and no Christianity Christian where the great Centralizing Power, the gravitation that binds every particle of Church and Life to Christ the Center, is robbed of its supremacy."[49] It was quite a performance. One wonders if there were those who resented his eloquence and his obvious authority.

Brooks moved out from this center into the world of culture, literature, and nature itself, seeking metaphors, models, and images that would illumine and in turn be illumined by the "real presence" he had discovered. He described the process himself: "The centre once set, the circle builds itself. The manifestation of the Son of God, of Christ, gives all other blessings a place and meaning, just as the sun in heaven accounts for and rescues from fragmentariness every little light of the innumerable host which, in every hue and brilliancy, sparkle and flash and glow from every point of our sun-lit world."[50] Then, as he remarked in the famous *Lectures on Preaching,* came the next step: close observation of the world around him. "I can remember how, as I looked forward to preaching, every book I read and every man I talked with seemed to teem with sermons. They all suggested something which it seemed as if the preacher of the Gospel ought to say to men. . . . I think there is not point in which ministers differ from one another . . . than in this—this open-mindedness and power of appropriating out of everything the elements of true instruction."[51]

But first there came immersion in the Bible. Brooks's method was to comb Scripture, constantly listing and commenting on texts that would show the relation of Jesus' death and resurrection to his teachings, to the events of his life, and, above all, to the theological significance of the Messiah, the Saviour and Redeemer. Brooks accepted it all and moved about freely in the biblical world. As a result of such freedom, figures of speech, individual characteristics, sayings, and parables presented themselves to him in profusion.

As he had gotten his own hand in and his ear tuned to the niceties of classical and contemporary verse, so now, as a theological student, Brooks began to listen seriously to the full score and cadences of the Bible. At first the "provincialisms" of the New Testament Greek pained his Boston Latin School ear. The style, he wrote, upon reading the New Testament in its original tongue, "is a conglomerate dialect, drawn not from Athens in the times of its power but from the Greek colonies in the time of Alexander and his successors." The New Testament authors "were generally men of low origin[; only] Luke & Paul were men of more education." The beginning of the Lucan corpus, according to Brooks, is "pure & classical, containing not one word or form which Plutarch might not have used as well." Otherwise the biblical Greek "had all the disadvantages of being a poor decayed tongue at best, used by men whose habits & associations lay in a language as different from it [classical Greek] as Moses was from Pericles."[52] His high standards notwithstanding, Brooks soon began to catch in the ancient, corrupted Greek of the texts the footfall of God's presence.

In the Bible, he wrote, "unseen powers as of reverence, love, life" become channels through which God comes to us. The movement was from God to humankind. Reflecting his reading in Tertullian and other church fathers, Brooks continued, "As the sun reaches the flower by heat spread through the atmosphere, so God reaches man by faith shed through life."[53] He proceeded on the essential religious persuasion that there is indeed an overarching moral and aesthetic design to the universe and that this design is to be seen in Jesus Christ. In him is the divine reality of God. To see him clearly and to make him seen, the preacher must pay attention to biblical particularities, above all sharpening his perceptions of Jesus' "personality." The result of Brooks's immersion in the Bible was that by the mid-1870s, when he began to prepare for the Bohlen Lectures at the Philadelphia Divinity School, there was—indeed, had been for some time—a freshness, a sense of surprise and delight, even astonishment, to the notes in which he recorded his first impressions of the Gospels. At times, however, these qualities did not carry over into the smoother, final text.

In what became the notebook of 1879, Brooks recorded his reflections in short, occasionally pithy aphorisms, each one accompanied by a shower of biblical references.[54] There was the "unity of his [Christ's] life"; a "fundamental reverence for Truth"; his use of "hyperboles—the giving of the cloak"; his "perception of the rudiments of intellectuality everywhere, Mark 4:12, Matthew 13:16"; his own "claim of personal Faithfulness, John 17:4, 15:10," and so forth; his "dealing with sorrow, John 11"; his lack of "unnatural stoicism [and] asceticism"; and the "self-discovery he brought" to others. Brooks noted that Jesus "seems always to appeal to what men might have known before or at any rate what might appeal to their natures once it was spoken." He commented on "the Encouragement & Discontent which Christ produces [in others]" and elsewhere wrote of "the Antagonisms which Christ excites. . . . Something of the same kind in Socrates." In Brooks's view we should examine "the value of such a condition in moral culture." He also wondered that there was no "element of humor" in the conveying of Christ's life as there had been in the case of Socrates: "None in Jesus and why? No Aristophanes ever undertook to make Jesus ridiculous *vide* The Clouds." He urged us to "compare Christ's talk to the disciples at the Last Supper with the Phaedo of Plato." And he kept returning to the two scenes: "The Phaedo closes with 'This was the end, Echecrates, of our friend, of all the men whom we have known the best & the wisest & most just'"—compared with Calvary, the end of the Phaedo was bland. The jailer who brought the poison to Socrates was compared to the Centurion at the foot of the cross. "The stronger drama," he concluded, was to be found in the New Testament. There Jesus dealt with Judas and washed his disciples' feet. Brooks noted in the New Testament accounts a "quickness of transition from good to evil so vehemently [reflected in] . . . Lessing's Faust fragment."[55]

As for the dramatic immediacy of the Bible, it was, in his opinion, enhanced by the element of the miraculous. "The value of miracles," he judged, was "in keeping the borders of life open." He also declared that the "whole condition & place of *miracles* [were] utterances of the nature of Jesus. Given his Being the miracles [are] not strange."[56]

On the subject of miracles, Brooks went beyond their instrumental and aesthetic value and took a position close to that of Edwards. He did so unwittingly, for there is no evidence that he had access to Edwards's private notebooks or that he ever read *The Distinguishing*

Marks of a Work of the Spirit of God. Had he done so, he would no doubt have approved. Both men approached the whole matter of the miraculous with caution. Edwards warned a too ardent age not to "give heed to such things" as "miraculous gifts in the approaching glorious times of the church." Expectations of wonderful and mysterious interventions, he declared, too often failed. Those who anticipate them leave "the sure word of prophecy, that God has given us to be a light shining in a dark place. . . . [They] leave the guidance of the pole star to follow a Jack-with-a-lanthorn . . . [in] a dreadful dance, and into woeful extravagancies."[57] Brooks, by contrast, had to deal with skepticism. And here he was most like Edwards when he moved beyond the immediate issue and gave full reign to the depth of his devotion. As Edwards had rejected the "extravagancies," Brooks rejected treating miracles as a matter first of all of "belief." Scripture did not so much bid the Christian believe in miracles as rejoice in the truth of Jesus Christ. Because the earth we tread "once trembled under the feet of Christ," Brooks declared, the Christian rejoices in God's acts and thereafter "is glad to believe."[58]

Both Edwards and Brooks thought of miracles in their relation to a neo-Platonic hierarchy of powers. Edwards was convinced that "if we ascend towards God in the scale of existence according to the degrees of excellency and perfection, the nearer we come to God, the nearer we shall come to the arbitrary influence of the Most High on the creature, till at length, when we come to the highest rank, we shall come [to] an intercourse that is, in many respects quite above those rules which we call the laws of nature."[59] But Brooks lacked Edwards's emphasis on the sovereignty of God. Instead of ascending to the One who is above and beyond all human cognition, Brooks focused on the descent of that One into human life and understanding. If God was in Christ, he judged, then miracles are "the natural and altogether to-be-expected utterances of [the life of Christ] in its reaction upon the material world." Moreover, "it would seem altogether likely that that life would have a peculiar relation to nature, perhaps a peculiar mode of entrance on the mortal career and a peculiar mode of departure from it, as well as peculiar power over it during the intervening years."[60]

As Edwards had described the superior powers of God in relation to the laws of Newtonian physics, Brooks described that power in relation to Darwinian biology:

I cannot but think also that the whole present tendency of physical science, which, with its theories of evolution, dwells upon the presence in the world of nature of a continually active formative force, is in the line of Christianity. Christ not merely taught that the divine Power was always at work in the world. He *was* Himself that present active divine power, and so, in some sense, not merely made miracles seem occasionally possible, but made all events seem miraculous, which is not the abolition of the idea of the miraculous any more than the flooding of the world with sunshine is an extinction of the sun.[61]

For Christians, following the polestar of the sense of Scripture, both Edwards and Brooks declared, was better than tripping after the jack-o'-lanterns of either the irrational or the skeptical. Moonshine and incredulity were both miscreant.

The Gospels revealed arresting characteristics to Brooks, for they seemed to touch human beings in all regions of their lives. Hence the New Testament was "a book with vast ideas impressed through [a] personal medium." In reading it, one was changed "with the felt fatherhood of God." Forgiveness of sin, new life, atonement were, according to Brooks, "all compressed under the Fatherhood" of God. He noted that in the Gospels "trial is not sin. . . . See the temptation [of Jesus in the wilderness], Matthew 4:1"; but, he added, "not hearing is a sin, Luke 10:10f." There was "a whole matter of the grade or rank of evil," that is, the distinctions among people made by Jesus (Luke 17:18). Brooks was also struck by what he called Jesus' "balance of Individualism and social life." He noted "the curious suggestion of Christ's *sociableness,* as the marriage at Cana, the feast in Levi's house, the talk about the 'son of man come eating and drinking.'"[62]

Brooks also noted the "difficult moral teachings, Luke 16:1[-13], Matthew 8:21[-22] and pointed out that Jesus was always interested in human motivations and responses. Christ seemed to place "greater emphasis on dispositions compared with positive and definite beliefs." In addition, he dealt with "the question of self-esteem . . . took the proud down without demoralizing them & lifted up the self-distrustful." Commenting on "Christ's courtesy, John 18:22–23," Brooks declared that courtesy—not answering back angrily—was more than respectability, which "is the ghost of duty." But the limits of Christ's patience, "where it breaks into impatience," fascinated him just as much. He wondered about masculinity and femininity in Jesus and noted Christ's emphasis on "women's rights."[63] Brooks was taken with the "instances of Jesus confusing, as it were, the temporal & spiritual, mercy, as in forgiveness of sins & healing of the palsied & how near together they lay in his mind." He recognized "Christ's apparent assignment of the lower motive 'agree with your adversary quickly, lest . . .'" He also showed a proper Bostonian's proper attitude to the woman taken in adultery: "Jesus often pretty loose & indulgent."[64]

When Jesus placed beauty and the good in the realm of human relationships, Brooks commented, he deliberately deepened those relationships, "knowing perfectly well the new and deeper pain that must come with profounder joy." Brooks wrote of the "manifest beauty of the combination of the intellectual and the spiritual in the gospels" and added that Christ democratized the intellectual by basing his teaching on the universal—and spiritual—fatherhood of God over his creatures, "and no man is excluded from it." There was Jesus' "calm assumption that all men could learn what he had to bestow."[65] Such knowledge was a matter of aesthetic and moral satisfaction; and in this vein Brooks declared elsewhere: "To come to Christ & grow like him is an enthusiastic and joyous labor that lights up eternity by anticipation with its endless pursuit of its infinite standard."[66]

For Brooks as well as for Edwards—and perhaps for Emerson too[67]— the aesthetic went hand in glove with the moral. Brooks did not seek to remove the aesthetic from the domain of practical morality or systematic cognition (after Kant's *Critique of Judgment*) but to show the intimate relation between the two. The question was which would dominate. Was Christ's morality a direct result of his beauty?—in which case a form of art might provide the metaphor by which one could come to the adoration of God. Or was Jesus Christ beautiful because he was moral?—in which case a pattern of character and conduct might invite emulation. In both Edwards and Brooks the moral and the aesthetic were intimately related, and one doubts whether either of them would have thought it worthwhile disentangling the two. Both qualities were encompassed in the person of Christ, who was himself the inspirer of "primary beauty" and "true virtue"—or, as Brooks put it, "the type of all humanity."[68]

This interrelation between the aesthetic and the moral rested on Brooks's desire to see the figure of Jesus of Nazareth as a single person and a "real presence." In an essay entitled "Biography," he wrote of his insistence on "seeing and knowing" the subject enshrined in the book: "Never lay a biography down until the man is a living, breathing acting person."[69] Whatever the technical difficulties of such advice with respect to the Gospels, while they are clearly not biographies in the modern sense, one thing is certain: Brooks read the New Testament as a drama that boasted the rarest of headliners. He would have agreed with Hans Frei's conclusion: "I am persuaded that historical inquiry is a useful and necessary procedure but that theological reading is the reading of a *text* and not of a *source*."[70]

• • •

With such a background we come to the preaching of Christ as Brooks developed that art. The New Englander forced his denomination for at least another two generations to retain the preached word as central to the act of worship and to the life of the church. He believed that the right words, emotionally and intellectually charged, could reach many and change their relationship to God and to each other. The assumption was, of course, that words, and particularly religious words, corresponded to what is, that language was still trustworthy, that logos and cosmos were inseparable, and that the covenant between rhetoric and reality was not yet broken (though it would be toward the end of the century). Not only may we trust what Jesus says is true, Brooks claimed, but a beautiful, "perfect" Christ so "glows" with God's justice that everything else "shines and burns with personal affection."[71] In other words, the transcendent Other comes to listeners through the artistry of the true preacher no less than through that of the painter, novelist, or musician. It is the daunting task of the preacher to awaken his auditors to such a reality, to let himself—and now herself—be used as a channel for the reality that brings him to this place.

It was in this frame of mind that in October 1858 Brooks resorted to private poetry before he preached the sermon "The Centralizing Power of the Gospel." Because of the trust that the age still had in the power of the spoken word, his verse is a revealing expression of his mind and heart. Absent the context we have examined, the following would seem sentimental and self-serving; in 1858 it was not:

> And so this sermon is my first;
> At last my hand has touched the plough,

And all my life o'er, blest or curst,
Is open wide before me now.

Well, let it come. With bended head
I turn this sermon to a prayer:
Lord, Thou hast marked my path to tread;
O, go with me and help me there.

In thy strength, not in mine I stand;
Thy words and not my own I speak;
In Thee my weakness waxeth grand,
And I am strong that was so weak.

So pass this sermon, if it must.
I think it pleads the truth of God.
I pray some soul will gather trust
To tread the path the Saviour trod.

Let other sermons follow too.
My way is marked, my path is clear,
A hope to win, a work to do,
In strength of faith, in spite of fear.

O God, whose name my soul has named,
O make them pure and all thine own,
That so I may not be ashamed,
When I shall stand before thy throne.[72]

In his application of Christology to preaching, Brooks argued that if only an *incarnate* God can speak of and convince another of the power of God, then only when that word is incarnate in preaching can God's word be spoken anew. We live by the truth of God in Jesus Christ, he declared, the one, simple truth that nonetheless is "marred and mangled by the multiplicity that is in man." But so long as the "intellect allows allegiance [to Christ], so long [as] its work is full of piety and purpose, its whole development is a training of the soul"— so long as, he might have added, we retain the conciseness, compactness, and completeness he thought he saw in Puritanism. For Brooks, singleness of purpose was everything. Thus he was led to say that Christ alone is the justice of God, he alone "glows with his [God's] justice in the eyes of men, a candle of the Lord."[73] As he wrote later: "Preaching Christ! That old phrase which has been so often the very watchword of cant—how it still declares the true nature of Christian teaching! Not Christianity but Christ! Not a doctrine, but a Person! Christianity only for Christ! The doctrine only for a Person!"[74]

In the God-man was what Brooks called the "glorious whole." It was made up of two parts, each of which invoked different aspects of the New England heritage. "Do I believe that Jonathan Edwards, when he has told me about the power and majesty of the divine will, has told me the whole truth?" he asked. "Do I believe on the other hand that [William Ellery] Channing, when he has told me of the purity and dignity of human nature, has told me the whole truth?" Edwards had revealed the deepest thought of one lost in God's existence. Channing was able to reveal man because he lived in "supreme sympathy with him." But, Brooks asked, "God and man, shall they stand separate?" The answer was no. His conclusion: "It is Christ, the God-man that I see."[75] Here was the preacher's central message. Phillips Brooks had at last found his ideal.

Conclusion

Phillips Brooks grew to young manhood in a time of changing American perception of the nation's identity and place in the world. Isolation began to give way to internationalism. Lewis Perry has remarked on the initial anti-British chauvinism "in the second quarter of the [nineteenth] century, [when] vast numbers of Americans cared little about England."[1] Worse, many of Brooks's fellow New Englanders saw the machinations of perfidious Albion in everything from abolitionism to the laying of the Atlantic telegraphic cable. As James Brewer Stewart points out, conservative Brahmins of Beacon Hill thought that abolitionism was simply "a confirmation of well-planned British plots to destroy civic harmony in Boston . . . [and initiate the] reenslavement of America."[2] In August 1858, William G. Brooks, Sr., recorded his own astonishment and delight in the exchange of greeting between Queen Victoria and President James Buchanan on the completion of the Atlantic cable. "Science has triumphed," wrote the elder Brooks; it was a "time of the greatest achievement." He then went on to ask, "who can tell what is to be the result of this great discovery? There are still many doubters who see nothing but trouble ahead in its use or its abuse, many who denounce it because it is in the hands of the English."[3]

For their part, abolitionists were marked by "blatant Anglophilia" and were internationalists as well.[4] The description fits Phillips

Brooks's emerging political attitude. The youth who steeped himself in English and continental history and literature would in the post-war years travel extensively in Europe, the Middle East, and Asia, preach in the great cathedrals of London, read widely in English and German theology, and make friends among the bishops and other clergy of the Church of England. As early as the 1850s he saved his choicest invective not for supposed British plots but, as his letters home show, for President Buchanan, the members of Congress, and the state officials in Richmond. He admired his polished, aristocratic, and radical cousin Wendell Phillips, who regularly castigated the commercial nabobs of Boston for their increasing southern orientation. He could not believe that his otherwise intelligent father had voted for Millard Fillmore in 1856. Unlike their father, the Brooks boys were ardent Republicans, antislavery advocates who made common cause with the "upper class rebels [who] defied conventions at every turn."[5]

As he became aware of the political world around him, whatever toll the disjointed times of the 1850s took on him, Brooks maintained a sense of purpose, even an exhilaration, in his outlook. Had he lived longer into the 1890s than he did, it might have been otherwise. As it was, Brooks died at just the right time. According to John Higham, a spirit of defeatism, the sense that religion was spiritually exhausted and that humankind was "the hapless plaything of great impersonal forces," came to dominate the intellectual climate of the 1890s. "The emergence of such an outlook," writes Higham, "was therefore a milestone in American intellectual history."[6] Brooks's optimism hardly fitted the new sense of helplessness. He was attracted to Arthur Schopenhauer's anti-Hegelian doctrine of the will,[7] but he had little in common with Algernon Charles Swinburne, the English aesthetes, or, had he lived long enough, the religious relativism of Harold Frederic or the somberness of Max Nordau's *Degeneration*.[8] There is no evidence that he ever read Giacomo Leopardi, the great classicist and purveyor of the early nineteenth-century philosophy of despair. Closer to home, his cousins Henry and Brooks Adams suffered from a certain sourness about the future that he certainly did not share.[9] What Brooks thought about the loss of hope in his fellow churchman E. L. Godkin of *The Nation* or in Mark Twain or even in William Dean Howells is a matter of conjecture. If at any time he felt displaced from his country and environment, we do not yet know it.

Brooks remained essentially hopeful and zestful to the end. Insofar as this was so, his ideal of the perfect person may be set beside the ideal of the perfect Christian home in the thinking of Harriet Beecher Stowe in *Uncle Tom's Cabin*,[10] or beside that of George Bancroft, Theodore Parker, and Abraham Lincoln with respect to the Declaration of Independence and its relationship to the Constitution.[11] In the writings of many of these men and women the influence of Coleridge and Carlyle brought German idealism to the study of American society, where "they saw the permanent ideal shining through the particulars of nature."[12] Brooks, their younger disciple, was no exception. He carried the beliefs of the optimists beyond mid-century and very nearly into the next one. At the same time, "the quiet erosion of inherited patterns of feeling, belief, and practice"[13] was taking place.

Unconscious recognition of that erosion may have been one factor in the crisis of Brooks's late adolescence, which has been part of this study. Indeed, that crisis of faith may well have precipitated Brooks's desire to search for the ideal in the first place. Not surprisingly, he found his guiding star and used its light to illumine his time in an effort to reverse the erosion of belief. In this effort he no doubt gained inspiration from Paul Rabaut's struggle against similar odds.

As we have seen, by sharply focusing attention on the figure of Jesus Christ, Brooks sought to make the dark walls of reality opaque. In his use of images—that of light comes readily to mind—he sought to make clear and simple the intention of Scripture itself. He absolutely identified Christianity with Christ, speaking more of Jesus' aesthetically inviting mode of virtue than of his unsubstitutable individuality made vivid by biblical event, parable, and circumstance. Insofar as this was so, he failed to explore sufficiently the singularity of the biblical narratives. Had Brooks read more carefully Calvin's *Institutes* or Luther's sermons, the Bible might have dominated his idealism rather than the other way around. Still, he remained surprisingly loyal to the reformed theology that he learned on his own and from others at Virginia Theological Seminary. He clearly meant to reflect its basic teachings about incarnation, atonement, justification, and sanctification. He also wanted that theology to be once more the common property of the men and women in the pews and not the private domain of academics, church bureaucrats, and seminarians.

One could say that Brooks was trilingual in the community of theological discourse. First, he had been brought up in an Episcopalian family. He attended an Episcopal seminary with a national reputation. He was typically Anglican in his reliance on the early church fathers, in his attention to eighteenth- and early nineteenth-century theologians of the Church of England, and in his engagement with the Episcopal liturgy throughout his youth, especially with the celebration of Christmas.[14] Second, he was influenced by the grammar of the larger culture, by the political and literary patterns of his day. With increasing awareness as he reached maturity, Brooks participated in republican nationalism and abolitionism, on the one hand, and in the romantic idealism set in motion by Shelley and Goethe, on the other. Unlike high-church Episcopalians, however, he neither distanced himself from those patterns nor sought refuge in "a small but distinct community in an alien environment."[15] Third, and perhaps most important, Brooks shared in the common theological and religious community of the longer—and larger—Christian tradition in general and of reformed Protestantism in particular. His reading of the works of Knapp, Hengstenberg, and Wayland, his interest in British and American Puritanism, together with his insistence on ceremonial simplicity in worship, attest to his investment in the common fund of evangelical and pietistic Protestantism. By his openness to and comprehension of other churches he sought to draw attention to those matters of faith that were shared by all of them.

Strengthening the public discourse of Protestantism in America meant for Brooks the avoidance of debate over ecclesiology, ceremony, and liturgy in his own denomination. These issues were playing a central role in the Episcopal church in the first twenty years of his ministry, and he found the debates distracting from his focus on the person of Jesus Christ. Brooks's primitivism, restorationism, call it by whatever name, had little appeal to those who sought a stronger denominational identity. In Anglo-Catholic circles this issue centered, popularly at least, on vestments and ceremony. Such matters appealed to the ritualists not simply for the sake of theatricality but because those forms, for them at least, spoke of the same longer Christian—but here medieval—tradition that Brooks himself demanded. Indeed, the outward forms of ceremony, sound, and even smell had their Christological purpose. They surrounded the person of Christ in the elements on the altar with an aura of beauty and mystery. Before that Lord, now incarnate in bread and wine, a reverent and disciplined people delighted to bend the knee in sincere obedience. Of course, such a ritual response distinguished Christ's Anglo-Catholic followers from the common Protestant herd with whom Brooks associated.

In the place and significance he gave to the sermon form, Brooks also exemplified a general Protestant tradition. Even the centrality of Christ within the oration itself can be said to reflect earlier Puritan conventions in American preaching.[16] By contrast, there was a decided shift in Brooks's homiletic art from the didactic to the personal and persuasive. The difference in artistic and psychological outlook between colonial America and the nineteenth century is primarily in the primacy of the individual in the Victorian era. With a heavy emphasis on "personality" and on the humanity of Jesus, the individual, initially apart from the community, came first in the scheme of things.

Nevertheless, Brooks had no quarrel with the old dictum *Ars est celare artem*.[17] Neither was he bent on impressing his hearers with his learning or with his artistic skill. He had no patience with preening homiletic technique. In January 1857 he wrote to his brother William that "students [at Virginia Theological Seminary] have imported an elocution teacher from Philadelphia who brags that he has taught Forest and Booth and all the great speakers of the country for the last twenty years. . . . [But] my limited means prevent my taking advantage of his instruction, and my taste and inclination would if my means didn't."[18] He was not the least impressed with how-to books on preaching. "Did you see Gresley on Preaching?" he asked his friend C. A. L. Richards. "Get it if you want the nearest finite thing to eternal stupidity."[19] Nor did he himself have any expectation of being a great preacher. On 3 February 1859, less than five months before his graduation from theological school, he wrote to his brother Frederick, who was then on a debating team at Harvard: "You know I never was much of a speaker. Lately I have been cultivating the extempore address & though no orator as Brutus is, yet it goes pretty glib & I expect to preach so a good deal of the time."[20] In the end he never did. He wrote out his sermons in full.

What made Brooks a great preacher was the clarity of his thinking, his freedom from apathy and routine, and the great wealth of reading he had done in the classics and in contemporary literature. He was energetic without being undisciplined, sincere without being sanctimonious, committed to his task without being intolerant of others, simple in speech without being simpleminded, and, above all, hopeful that he could release those who were trapped by closed patterns of order. He was not an apologist and did not engage modern thought except indirectly. The Gospel of Christ, he assumed, stood on its own merits; it had its own intention, consistency, and way of speaking. It was not so much that Brooks rejected the doctrines of evangelicalism as he refused to argue or state them as doctrines. By going to their source, the Christ of the Gospels, he "restated" them in a new way. And in so doing he did not have to become a "fundamentalist," for he already had a clear idea of what was fundamental.

Insofar as he was thus engaged, Brooks came to transcend the narrow sectionalism of his region. As we have seen, as an Episcopalian he made no claims for the superiority of his church over others. In his denomination he led no church party. In the pulpit he seemed above theological controversy.[21] He appealed broadly across the American nation to those not content with the "passionate rejection of the past," which, as Nathan Hatch has observed, was one of the marks of the genius of the Second Great Awakening.[22] Brooks continued the Puritan tradition of high culture, particularly the enduring spirituality of the New England pulpit. Insofar as he did this he must be placed beside the New Divinity leaders who sought to moderate the Methodization of evangelical Christianity.[23]

If Brooks maintained the plain style of his ancestors, the architectural setting in which he achieved his greatest fame was anything but simple. After fire destroyed his parish, a new Trinity Church was built in the center of Boston's fashionable Back Bay. The building, begun in 1873 by wealthy parishioners, was not completed until 9 February 1877. Its elegant doors were opened just five months before the Great Strike ushered in two decades of the most vicious class warfare America had ever known. And that was not the only contrast. Trinity was a far cry from the Whiggish simplicity of either Puritan or Episcopalian evangelicalism.[24] The new house of worship was the work of friends of Henry Adams: the great architect Henry H. Richardson, the interior designer Stanford White, and the artist John La-Farge. In the construction of what became one of America's most magnificent buildings, no effort was spared. In 1884 Adams himself wrote a thinly disguised novel, *Esther,* about the building of Trinity Church and about its remarkable minister.

The church's largely, though by no means exclusively, Franco-Spanish Romanesque style marked a reaction on Richardson's and Brooks's part against the Anglo-Catholic revival of Gothic architecture and in favor of what was then thought to be a purer style. The openness of the interior space under the massive central tower allowed little or no distinction between those areas reserved for the clergy and those for the laity. Proximity, if not intimacy, was achieved even in this vast auditorium. The primacy of the preached Word of God was evident in the massive pulpit with its majestic sounding board. The peoples' communion around most of a freestanding holy table rather than the ceremonial and sacramental action of the priest, protected by a rood screen, was made evident in the unobstructed access of the laity to the spacious chancel. Trinity symbolized for its builders the hoped-for renewal of Protestant worship.

The beauty of Trinity's architecture, its moldings, its wall paintings, and its dim, religious light were also rich and romantic. As much as in the Anglo-Catholic cathedrals of Ralph Adams Cram, the new Trinity Church was a house of worship for those who not only took "both their morality and their theology seriously"[25] but did so in the expectation that both would be served up with style and even sublimity. It was not so much a matter of enjoying the fruits of material affluence or of affirming the respectability of industrial capitalism as making the religious revival acceptable to a more cosmopolitan and even theatrical taste of a new generation that assumed it was more sophisticated than the last. The religious convictions of the 1870s and 1880s need not be reduced to either production or consumption. Ferdinand Ewer remarked that ritualistic services generated "unspeakable awe, derived from the realization of the supernatural"—hitherto, it was thought, by many and unavailable to Protestant Episcopalians.[26]

If the ceremonial of candles, stained glass, vestments, incense, and solemn manual acts of consecration made the supernatural visible in Anglo-Catholic parishes, Brooks made it "speakable." In a somber generation, bowed down by the terrible losses of the Civil War, his transformed Protestantism offered hope. It did so by preserving a sense of the miraculous and then linking it with the everyday. Put slightly differently, Brooks was able to convey his own enchantment with Scripture and the world around him. Bound together by his art, they revealed the world that really was.[27] Christ was not alone incarnate upon the altars but seemed to speak directly to people from Trinity's broad, stagelike pulpit. Through the words of the preacher, uttered in the great theater of that church, Brooks spoke simply and convincingly. As Charles Hopkins observed, the moderated Calvinism "preached by Beecher, Phillips Brooks, Washington Gladden, and other progressive ministers . . . retained a strong supernaturalism and insisted [also] upon the primacy of individual character."[28] At the same time Richardson's espousal of "homiletical mediation" filled the longing for new spiritual capability. Like his Anglo-Catholic opponents, Brooks also understood the impoverishment of industrial, secular culture.[29]

Sharply attuned to his surroundings early in his life, Brooks came to maturity at the beginning of the greatest crisis in American history. As he struck out on his own in 1856, the political turbulence that swirled around him played its inevitable role. The menace of the approaching conflict, stormy sectional rivalries, personal insecurity, and flimsy institutional protection conduced to make the going rough. But instead of distraction and despair, he struggled all the harder to achieve scarcely understood aims and goals. The changes occurring in society forced him to expand his mind and at the same time to discriminate. Shaken by personal defeat, homesick in a strange part of the country with which he had little sympathy, initially immature, tentative about his commitments, yet sure of himself intellectually at least, he mastered a considerable body of theological and scholarly literature. He drew no line between intellectuality and spirituality. At the same time he devised new ways of presenting the central figure of Christian faith. If the times were not heroic, that was all the more reason to proclaim the hero he found. In doing so he brought the Episcopal church closer to the tradition of Protestantism out of which it sprang. That his church increasingly found itself ambivalent about that tradition does not detract from his accomplishment or from his challenge to it. The accomplishment was his restatement and representation of the centrality of Christ. The challenge to those who would hear was to shape their individual characters morally and aesthetically in the light of Christ's perfect personhood, which was as pure as it was beautiful. Here alone was truth to be found.

A universe of parts and "little things," as Coleridge had suggested in 1797, was unendurable. The poet's mind ached to behold "something *one & individual.*"[30] As he came to maturity in the 1850s in a society on the brink of civil chaos, Phillips Brooks beheld this One Thing. Thereafter he relayed what he had seen to his generation.

. . .

For all these reasons, and because he pursued his quest indefatigably and independently, Brooks became one of the two great Anglican preachers in America. The other—in the previous century—was George Whitefield. Comparison is neither fortuitous nor ill conceived: both men had roots in the theology of England's sixteenth-century reformers and in the Articles of Religion those reformers produced; both preached with stunning directness; both shared a vivid personal faith; both fitted themselves into the narrative of Scripture.[31] While Whitefield allied himself with the eighteenth-century American Puritan clergy, Brooks, as has been shown, was not unaware of his Puritan roots and maintained close ties throughout his career with ministers and laity of other denominations. Both men incurred the dislike of those who worked for an Anglican identity separate from that of what they imagined was American Protestantism in general. In both cases high churchmen were by no means reluctant to campaign against them—in Whitefield's case, at the beginning of his ministry; in Brooks's, at the end of it, when Anglo-Catholics tried to keep him from being approved as bishop of Massachusetts. On both men the denominational label was in the end barely readable. It has been held to his credit—by some—that when Brooks died, thousands of his fellow countrymen and women were unaware that he was an Episcopalian.

In the larger catalog of great American preachers, Brooks ranks with his ancestor John Cotton. In his own time, he was as renowned as William Ellery Channing, Henry Ward Beecher, Horace Bushnell, Dwight L. Moody, and DeWitt Talmage. In the beauty of his language, Brooks was perhaps more lasting than any of them. For the power and intensity of his addresses, one would place him alongside Edwards, Emerson, Reinhold Niebuhr, and Martin Luther King, Jr. William B. Lawrence remarks on the thoughtful, scholarly character of Brooks's sermons and goes on to say: "His influence on preaching in America is almost immeasurable. . . . [He] defined preaching as the proclamation of truth through personality, and no better description has been offered since."[32] Harriet Beecher Stowe, who became an Episcopalian in 1864, may be excused a degree of sentimentality when, on hearing of Brooks's death, she remarked: "Since the going home of my dear brother Henry [Ward Beecher] our country has not sustained such a loss as this of Phillips Brooks. He was one of the truly great ones of this earth,—great in the noble simplicity of his life and character."[33] No better description of Brooks than Stowe's "noble simplicity"—with or without artistry—has been offered since.

Despite such praise, the final theological word—at least of this study of Brooks—must be quite critical. "From the vantage point of later history," writes Roger Lundin, "romanticism [we must include Brooks in this mind-set] appears as a transitional movement, a stage on the way from the magical and sacramental world of the late Middle Ages to the desacralized world of modernity."[34] Having spurned the rationalism and empiricism of the Enlightenment, Romantics were nonetheless intent on pursuing the goals of the Enlightenment: the understanding of the self and its relationship to nature, authority, and tradition. They were optimistic, even utopian, about their ability to know that self and to discover in the world around them truth and secure principles. Time has been unkind to them. The horrors of the twentieth century, its savage slaughters of whole peoples, its cynicism about governments and their self-seeking motives, and its despair over the vast new powers placed in the hands of lawless individuals mock enlightened and romantic assertions of human goodness. The claims of such Romantics as Brooks about the powers of human consciousness appear naïve. The individual self they placed at the center of attention—rather than the historic community—has come to be seen as having no inherent truth within it to disclose.[35] As a result, writes Lundin,

> interpretation can do no more than document the power of desire in language, and apologetics is left with the sad task of pouring contemporary experience into the hollow shell of empty Christian language. In this scheme of things interpretation is reduced to the art of helping the self achieve satisfaction by all available means. For those who believe that religious language refers to nothing more than various stages or aspects of the self, therapy supplants truth as the goal of understanding, and theology becomes a mere footnote to the primary text of anthropology.[36]

Brooks would have been horrified at such an outcome; nor can we hold him responsible for the contemporary emasculation of historic and communal Christian faith. Certainly, for him the stories in the Bible did far more than illuminate our individual struggles. For him

Scripture was more than a record of human aspiration and oppression—possibly to the exclusion of much else. If only Brooks had sided more with Edwards than with Channing! What the Christian looks for in creation, remarks Lundin, "is something greater than the stunning reflection of his or her own desiring countenance." That something is the Word of God, which "is more than an echo of his or her own clamoring voice."[37] Were this not so, then we Christians, as St. Paul remarked, "are of all men most to be pitied" (1 Corinthians 15:19).

Notes

Introduction

1. See Alexander V. G. Allen, *Life and Letters of Phillips Brooks,* 2 vols. (New York: E. P. Dutton, 1900), 2:930–40, for an account of Brooks's death. On the basis of the evidence, there seems to be no doubt that the diagnosis of diphtheria, made at the time, is correct (letter from Peter B. Hope, M.D., to John Woolverton, 10 Jan. 1994).

2. *New York Times,* 27 Jan. 1893, 10.

3. Marlene Deahl Merrill, ed., *Growing Up in Boston's Gilded Age: The Journal of Alice Stone Blackwell, 1872–1874* (New Haven: Yale University Press, 1990), 58–59.

4. Ibid., 182.

5. The Bishop of Springfield [George Seymour], *An Open Letter to the Rt. Rev. William C. Doane . . . in Reference to the Consecration of the Rt. Rev. Dr. Brooks . . .* (Springfield, Ill.: H. W. Rokker, 1892), 19. See also J. B. M. Frederick, "George Franklin Seymour, A.M., S.T.D, D.C.L, LL.D, Second Dean of the General Theological Seminary and First Bishop of Springfield" (B.D. thesis, St. Mark's Library, General Theological Seminary, New York, 1954).

6. Seymour, *Open Letter,* 10. On Brooks's attitudes, see Raymond W. Albright, *Focus on Infinity: A Life of Phillips Brooks* (New York: Macmillan, 1961), 362.

7. See, for instance, Diana Hochstedt Butler, "Standing against the Whirlwind: The Evangelical Party in the Nineteenth-Century Protestant Episcopal Church" (Ph.D. diss., Duke University, 1991), 97, 102, 103, 104.

8. Phillips Brooks, *Essays and Addresses* (New York: E. P. Dutton, 1894), 202.

9. See John 15, esp. verses 12–13.

10. George F. Seymour, *The Church of Rome in Her Relation to Christian Unity Both in the Falsity of Papal Claims or Romanism Not Catholicism* (London: W. Spreaight and Sons, 1889), 19.

11. George F. Seymour, *Sermon Preached at the Consecration of Thomas F. Gailor as Bishop Coadjutor of Tennessee* (Milwaukee: Young Churchman Co., 1895), 21.

12. See, for instance, Herbert J. Muller, *Religion and Freedom in the Modern World* (Chicago: University of Chicago Press, 1963), 82; William A. Clebsch, *From Sacred to Profane America: The Role of Religion in American History* (New York: Harper and Row, 1968), 212; and R. Laurence Moore, *Religious Outsiders and the Making of Americans* (New York: Oxford University Press, 1986).

13. George F. Seymour, *The Historic Episcopate: A Contribution towards Church Unity* (New York: Church Unity Society, 1892), 8, 11.

14. Seymour, *Open Letter*, 12.

15. See T. J. Jackson Lears, *No Place of Grace: Antimodernism and the Transformation of American Culture, 1880–1920* (New York: Pantheon, 1981), 198–203.

16. Seymour, *Open Letter*, 11.

17. [George F. Seymour], *The Untruthfulness of the Age: Danger Signals* (New York, 1894), 11.

18. In the Episcopal church bishops are elected by constitutional majorities of the clergy and laity of a diocese, voting by orders in their diocesan conventions. If the election takes place within three months of a General Convention of the entire denomination, the necessary testimonials are forwarded to the secretary of the House of Deputies (made up of clerical and lay people elected from all dioceses) for their vote. The House of Bishops then votes in similar fashion and conveys the result to the standing committee of the electing diocese. (Standing committees, made up of clergy and laity, are counsels of advice to bishops; in the absence of bishops, standing committees are the ecclesiastical authorities.)

When an election occurs more than three months before the next triennial General Convention, a majority of the standing committees of the several dioceses must assent to consecration along with a majority of all bishops. This was the process that took place in Brooks's case. See E. A. White and J. A. Dyckman, *Annotated Constitution and Canons for the Government of the Protestant Episcopal Church*, 2 vols. (New York: Seabury Press, 1982; New York: Office of the General Convention, 1985), 2:693–94, 717.

19. Albright, *Focus,* 364, 365. The Anglo-Catholic camp was itself divided, and A. C. A. Hall, the leader of the Society of St. John the Evangelist, supported Brooks's consecration once he had been elected. For this Hall was disciplined by his superiors in England (376–77).

20. Horace E. Scudder, "The Contributors' Club," *Atlantic Monthly,* Dec. 1877, 751.

21. Allen, *Life and Letters,* 2:814; 2:20, 21; 2:9–10; 2:807.

22. William Lawrence, *Phillips Brooks: A Study* (Boston: Houghton Mifflin, 1903), 5, 36.

23. Eliot, Lee, and Huntington are all quoted in Bayard S. Clark, "A Sermon by Phillips Brooks on the Death of Abraham Lincoln," *Historical Magazine of the Protestant Episcopal Church* 49, no. 1 (Mar. 1980), 38. No manuscript has ever been found of Brooks's prayer. His father merely recorded in his diary that "five hundred and twenty-eight of the graduates joined the army. Ninety-three lost their lives. The celebration today has been one of the best and most successful I ever knew; having received a complimentary ticket on account of the death of George [Phillips's younger brother] I attended all day. The services at the church were [?], a prayer by son Phillips and an Oration by the Rev. Mr. Putnam of Roxbury—all exceedingly interesting" (Diaries of W. G. Brooks, Sr., 1838–77, William Gray Brooks Papers, Massachusetts Historical Society, Boston; Diary, 1863–66, 1101). George Brooks died of typhoid fever on 10 January 1863 in New Bern, North Carolina, where he was serving with the 45th Massachusetts (Allen, *Life and Letters,* 1:420).

24. In *Fifty Years* (Boston: Houghton Mifflin, 1923), 35, William Lawrence speaks of Brooks's "flashing eye . . . as, standing by the lectern pulpit in Huntington Hall [in the early 1870s], he lifted the people to . . . a spiritual conception of the inspiration of the Old Testament."

25. Henry Adams, *The Education of Henry Adams* (Boston: Houghton Mifflin, 1918), 315. Adams's novel *Esther* (1884; New York: Literary Classics of the United States, 1983), originally written under the pseudonym Frances Snow Compton, is a thinly veiled account of Brooks as the champion of religion in a scientific age. Adams's not unsympathetic view is echoed by Henry Steele Commager, who remarked, incorrectly as it turns out, "After Phillips Brooks no Protestant churchman spoke with authority" (*The American Mind* [New Haven: Yale University Press, 1950], 167. Commager might well wish to revise his judgment to include Reinhold Niebuhr and Martin Luther King, Jr. The omission of Mark Twain from Adams's list is less excusable.

26. Henry F. May, *The Protestant Churches and Industrial America* (New York: Harper and Brothers, 1949), 64, 65, 66.

27. Winthrop Hudson, *Religion in America,* 3d ed. (New York:

Charles Scribner's Sons, 1981), 307, 374. In *The Great Tradition of the American Churches* (New York: Harper and Brothers, 1953), 163, Hudson notes that Brooks's national and international reputation had rarely been equaled.

28. Martin E. Marty, *Righteous Empire: The Protestant Experience in America* (New York: Dial Press, 1970), 191, 149. See also Lears, *No Place of Grace*, 24. These views should be tempered—but were not—by the influence of William S. Rainsford, the Irish socialist rector of St. George's Church in New York, whose long friendship with Brooks is recorded in his book *The Story of a Varied Life* (1922; Freeport, N.Y.: Books for Libraries Press, 1970), 166, 184–85, 212, 295–96. In addition, Brooks's sermon "Christian Charity" reveals a mind capable of vivid portrayal of the plight of the urban poor even while patronizing them (in *The Candle of the Lord* [New York: E. P. Dutton, 1895], 336–54).

29. Sydney E. Ahlstrom, *A Religious History of the American People* (New Haven: Yale University Press, 1972), 739.

30. Lears, *No Place of Grace*, 23, 209. See also William Warren Sweet, *The Story of Religion in America* (1930; New York: Harper and Brothers, 1950), who does not mean to be derogatory of Brooks but notes his lack of original thought: Brooks's "catching up the finest spiritual ideas of his time and putting them into glowing words" appears to a more critical age to damn with faint praise (386).

31. Donald Fleming, "Eliot's New Broom," *Glimpses of Harvard's Past* (Cambridge: Harvard University Press, 1986), 76–77.

32. William B. Lawrence, "The History of Preaching in America," *Encyclopedia of the American Religious Experience,* ed. Charles H. Lippy and Peter W. Williams, 3 vols. (New York: Charles Scribner's Sons, 1988), 3:1307–24, 1318.

33. Albright, *Focus.*

34. Phillips Brooks, *The Joy of Preaching* (Grand Rapids, Mich.: Kregel Publications, 1989). The volume comprises Brooks's famous Lyman Beecher Lectures delivered at Yale University in 1877.

35. Warren W. Wiersbe, "Introduction," in ibid., 20. On Brooks's doctrine of the atonement, Wiersbe writes: "At times, he seemed to hold to a 'moral influence' theory of the atonement, but later he would boldly affirm a more orthodox position" (18).

36. Marc Pachter, "The Biographer Himself: An Introduction," in *Telling Lives: The Biographer's Art,* ed. Marc Pachter (Washington, D.C.: New Republic Books, 1979), 12.

37. Ibid., 6.

38. See Erich Auerbach, *Mimesis: The Representation of Reality in Western Literature* (Princeton: Princeton University Press, 1953), chap.

2, esp. 40–49, for a description of the eclipse of the style of antique tragedy by the dynamic, figural meaning of New Testament texts.

39. William Stringfellow, *A Simplicity of Faith* (Nashville: Abingdon Press, 1982), 19–20.

Chapter 1: New England Religion and Doting Parents

1. Harry S. Stout, *The New England Soul: Preaching and Religious Culture in Colonial New England* (New York: Oxford University Press, 1986), 312.

2. Lester H. Cohen, "Creating a Usable Future: The Revolutionary Historians and the National Past," in *The American Revolution: Its Character and Limits,* ed. Jack P. Greene (New York: New York University Press, 1987), 313.

3. Nathan O. Hatch, "In Pursuit of Religious Freedom: Church, State, and People in the New Republic," in *The American Revolution,* ed. Greene, 393. See also Hatch, *The Democratization of American Christianity* (New Haven: Yale University Press, 1989), esp. 112, 128, 179.

4. Calvin Colton, *The Genius and Mission of the Protestant Episcopal Church* (New York: Stanford and Swords, 1853), 224, 237, 228. For a discussion of Colton's position, see Robert Bruce Mullin, *Episcopal Vision/American Reality: High Church Theology and Social Thought in Evangelical America* (New Haven: Yale University Press, 1986), 118–19, 123–24, 179–80. As Mullin points out, Colton was equally opposed to the revivalist measures of Charles Grandison Finney (119).

5. See Butler, "Standing against the Whirlwind, 249.

6. Colleen McDannell, *The Christian Home in Victorian America, 1840–1900* (Bloomington: Indiana University Press, 1986), esp. chap. 6 and 151–52.

7. For the downplaying of interest in doctrine, see Ann Douglas, *The Feminization of American Culture* (New York: Avon Books, 1977), chap. 4, esp. 168–69. See also McDannell, *Christian Home,* 18, with reference to the lack of interest in reform theology.

8. See Cleveland Amory, *The Proper Bostonians* (New York: E. P. Dutton, 1947), 65; see also *Dictionary of American Biography,* s.v. "Peter Chardon Brooks."

9. Richard Hofstadter, *Anti-Intellectualism in American Life* (New York: Alfred A. Knopf and Random House, 1962), 247.

10. The term was coined by Stow Persons in *The Decline of American Gentility* (New York: Columbia University Press, 1973).

11. Daniel Walker Howe, "Victorian Culture in America," in *Victo-*

rian America, ed. Daniel Walker Howe (Philadelphia: University of Pennsylvania Press, 1976), 12.

12. Ibid., 160.

13. So-called for Samuel Hopkins, successor to Jonathan Edwards, who, along with Joseph Bellamy in the later eighteenth century, systematized Edwards's thought and won a following in American Calvinism. Hopkins and the "New Divinity" theologians emphasized sin as self-love and regeneration as issuing in selflessness or disinterested charity or benevolence, and thereby opened the door for a postmillenial social gospel. See Joseph A. Conforti, *Samuel Hopkins and the New Divinity Movement* (Grand Rapids, Mich.: Christian University Press, 1981).

14. James McLachlan, *American Boarding Schools: A Historical Study* (New York: Charles Scribner's Sons, 1970), 40. For a discussion of the founding of Phillips Academy, Andover, and of Phillips Exeter Academy, see ibid., chap. 1.

15. Mary's great-great-grandfather Samuel Phillips, for sixty-two years minister of the South Church, remained "steadfast in adherence to the Westminster Catechism" (Allen, *Life and Letters,* 1:8). For a discussion of the emergence of Unitarianism in New England, see Peter W. Williams, "Unitarianism and Universalism," *Encyclopedia of the American Religious Experience,* ed. Lippy and Williams, 1:580–81.

16. I am indebted to Dr. Robert D. Stevens of North Andover, Massachusetts, for this information gleaned from North Parish Church records and conveyed to me in a conversation on 17 February 1994.

17. Albright quotes the journal of the Episcopal rector John Stone of St. Paul's Church in Boston to the effect that both Mary and her sister Susan were "members of ye Unitarian Church in North Andover" (*Focus,* 16). Stone, we now know, was incorrect in the case of Mary.

18. Mary Brooks to Phillips Brooks, 27 Nov. 1864, quoted in Allen, *Life and Letters,* 1:262–63.

19. See Horace Bushnell, "The Vicarious Sacrifice," in *Horace Bushnell,* ed. H. Shelton Smith (New York: Oxford University Press, 1965), 276–310, esp. 297–98, in which Jesus is seen as both redeemer and example. For Bushnell's mature doctrine of the work of Christ, see "Forgiveness and the Law," in ibid., 310–74, esp. 316–17, 323–28, 331–33.

20. Mary Brooks to Phillips Brooks, 27 Nov. 1864, quoted in Allen, *Life and Letters,* 1:262–63.

21. Brooks, *The Joy of Preaching,* 33. Isaac Barrow, seventeenth-century Anglican royalist divine, was successively professor of Greek and mathematics at Cambridge University and one of the most famous preachers of his day. The sermons of John Tillotson, archbishop of Canterbury, became models for English and American preaching in the eigh-

teenth century. See W. M. Spellman, "Archbishop John Tillotson and the Meaning of Moralism," *Anglican and Episcopal History* 56, no. 4 (Dec. 1987), 404–22.

22. William G. Brooks, Sr., Diary, 1838–42, 4.

23. Emerson is quoted in Henry Steele Commager, *Theodore Parker* (Boston: Beacon Press, 1947), 77.

24. Earl Morse Wilber, *A History of Unitarianism in Transylvania, England, and America* (Cambridge: Harvard University Press, 1952), 439. See also Octavius Brooks Frothingham, *Boston Unitarianism* (Boston: G. P. Putnam's, 1890), 97.

25. For the text of Emerson's address, see Sydney E. Ahlstrom, *Theology in America: The Major Protestant Voices from Puritanism to Neo-Orthodoxy* (Indianapolis: Bobbs-Merrill, 1967), 293–316. For the address's place in Emerson's thought, see William A. Clebsch, *American Religious Thought: A History* (Chicago: University of Chicago Press, 1973), 80–83.

26. William G. Brooks, Sr., Diary, 1838–42, 33. See also E. Clowes Chorley, *Men and Movements in the American Episcopal Church* (New York: Charles Scribner's Sons, 1946), 55. Stone was the author of *Memoir of the Life of Rt. Rev. Alexander Viets Griswold, D.D.* (Philadelphia: Stavely and McCalla, 1844).

27. William G. Brooks, Sr., Diary, 1838–42, 33.

28. William G. Brooks, Sr., Diary, 1846–49, 254, 255.

29. William G. Brooks, Sr., Diary, 1838–42, 69; Diary, 1846–49, 284.

30. Alan M. Kantrow, "Anglican Custom, American Consciousness," *New England Quarterly* 52, no. 3 (Sept. 1979), 315, quoting George Keith, *Mr. Keith's Farewell Sermon* (London: W. Bowyer, 1700).

31. See John F. Woolverton, *Colonial Anglicanism in North America, 1607–1776* (Detroit: Wayne State University Press, 1984), 177.

32. Kantrow, "Anglican Custom," 312.

33. Ibid., 309.

34. George L. Blackman and Mark J. Duffy, "The Tradition of Massachusetts Churchmanship," in *The Episcopal Diocese of Massachusetts, 1784–1984,* ed. Mark J. Duffy (Barnstable: Episcopal Diocese of Massachusetts, 1984), 13. The Anglo-Catholic presence in Boston was not evident until the founding of the Church of the Advent in 1844. I found no comments about this church or about the Oxford Movement in either the papers of William G. Brooks, Sr., or of Phillips Brooks, at least not until after the Civil War and then, in Phillips Brooks's case, largely on ritualism.

35. Butler, "Standing against the Whirlwind," 62.

36. Beecher sat on the fence on this one, while Bushnell denied total

depravity. See H. Shelton Smith, *Changing Conceptions of Original Sin: A Study in American Theology since 1750* (New York: Charles Scribner's Sons, 1955), 131–33, 159–60.

37. Ibid., 56.

38. The Brooks boys and their dates of birth: William Gray, Jr. (1834), Phillips (1835), George (1838), Frederick (1842), Arthur (1845), and John Cotton (1849).

39. Anne C. Rose, *Victorian America and the Civil War* (Cambridge: Cambridge University Press, 1992), 7.

40. James McPherson, *The Battle Cry of Freedom: The Civil War Era* (New York: Oxford University Press, 1988), 35.

41. Allen, *Life and Letters,* 1:46. I do not find evidence, in this case at least, that the pious feelings engendered by learning hymns "overshadowed the message of such conventional forms as the Bible and sermons" (Rose, *Victorian America,* 21).

42. Allen, *Life and Letters,* 1:46.

43. See E. Anthony Rotundo, "Boy Culture: Middle-Class Boyhood in Nineteenth-Century America," in *Meanings for Manhood: Constructions for Masculinity in Victorian America,* ed. Mark C. Carnes and Clyde Griffen (Chicago: University of Chicago Press, 1990), 17.

44. Albright, *Focus,* 13.

45. William G. Brooks, Sr., to Phillips Brooks, 4 Jan. 1859, Phillips Brooks Papers, bMS AM 1594.1, (635), box 41, Houghton Library, Harvard University; Mary Brooks to Phillips Brooks, 20 Oct. 1857, bMS AM 1594.1, (39), folder 1. See also William G. Brooks, Sr., to Phillips Brooks, 11 Feb. 1858, bMS AM 1594.1, (40), folder 1, on Alexander Vinton's "detestable habit of smoking." Phillips went on smoking cigars for the rest of his life.

46. Mary Brooks to Phillips Brooks, 19 Mar. 1859, bMS AM 1594.1, (41), folder 1. See also Mary Brooks to Phillips Brooks, 2 Jan., 10 Jan., and 20 Nov. 1858, all in bMS AM 1594.1, (41), folder 1.

47. Mary Brooks to Phillips Brooks, 20 Nov. 1859, quoted in Allen, *Life and Letters,* 1:281. See also Mary Brooks to Phillips Brooks, 5 Oct. 1858, bMS AM 1594.1, (40), folder 3.

48. William G. Brooks, Sr., to Phillips Brooks, 29 Nov. 1858, bMS AM 1594.1, (40), folder 3.

49. Mary Brooks, 1 July 1859, in Mary Ann Phillips Brooks, "Notes concerning the Confirmation and Ordination of Phillips Brooks A MS; Dorchester & [n.p.] 2 Jul 1857 & 1 Jul 1859," bMS AM 2022, (143).

50. Phillips Brooks to Dr. S. Weir Mitchell, Feb. 1880, quoted in Allen, *Life and Letters,* 2:252.

51. Quoted in Allen, *Life and Letters,* 2:256. Allen declares that the

quote comes not from Mary but from someone who heard her speak along such lines.

52. William G. Brooks, Sr., to Phillips Brooks, 12 Dec. 1859, bMS AM 2022, (39), folder 2.

53. Rose, *Victorian America*, 8.

54. Albright, *Focus*, 212.

55. See Richard Lebeaux, *Young Man Thoreau* (Amherst: University of Massachusetts Press, 1977), esp. 45–46.

56. William G. Brooks, Sr., to Phillips Brooks, [Spring?] 1859, quoted in Allen, *Life and Letters*, 2:254. Mary also worried about her son's eyesight (Mary Brooks to Phillips Brooks, "c. 1858," bMS AM 1594.1, [40], folder 1). Cf. Mary Brooks to Phillips Brooks, 19 Feb. and 3 Mar. 1858, bMS AM 1594.1, (40), folder 1.

57. William G. Brooks, Sr., Diary, 1853–57, 501.

58. Ibid., 501–2.

59. Ibid., 502.

60. Phillips Brooks to George Brooks, 23 Dec. 1857, bMS AM 2022, (26), folder labeled "6 letters to George Brooks ([1857]–1862)."

61. William G. Brooks, Sr., Diary, 1846–49, 355.

62. See, for instance, Phillips's emphasis on the "sense of personal responsibility" and on "deliberateness" in *Joy of Preaching*, 128, 129.

63. William was an acknowledged and expert penman, a fair artist; his son, whose handwriting closely resembled his own, was a careful, if uninspired, sketcher. Phillips was also good at making things—kites for his younger brothers—and even at sewing, which at one point worried his father, who thought it effeminate.

64. William G. Brooks, Sr., Diary, 1853–57, 507.

65. William G. Brooks, Sr., to Phillips Brooks, 21 Dec. 1857, bMS AM 1594.1, (39), folder 2.

66. William G. Brooks, Sr., Diary, 1846–49, 207. On 11 August 1834, a mob of anti-Catholics stormed the front door of the Ursuline Convent while the nuns, with the children under their care (mostly Unitarians), fled out the back. The convent was then burned to the ground. Lyman Beecher's inflammatory sermons were partly to blame. See Ray Allen Billington, *The Protestant Crusade, 1800–1860: A Study of the Origins of American Nativism* (New York: Rinehart, 1938), 70, 72–73.

67. William G. Brooks, Sr., Diary, 1846–49, 209. It should be noted that these comments were made before the alliance in the 1850s between State Street's die-hard Whigs and the Irish conservatives, who became allies against the Free-Soil party and the Democrats, who supported a new constitution for Massachusetts. See Oscar Handlin, *Boston's Immigrants, 1790–1880*, 3d ed. (New York: Atheneum, 1968), 191–97.

68. William G. Brooks, Sr., Diary, 1846–49, 227.

69. William G. Brooks, Sr., Diary, 1838–42, 140–41.

70. William G. Brooks, Sr., Diary, 1853–57, 693.

71. William G. Brooks, Sr., Diary, 1858–61, 803.

72. William G. Brooks, Sr., Diary, 1838–42, 71.

73. William G. Brooks, Diary, 1853–57, 379. Stowe went to England at the invitation of the antislavery aristocracy, and her months there were a triumph. There was hardly anyone of prominence she and her husband, Calvin, failed to meet, except for Queen Victoria, whom she met on subsequent trips. See Harriet Beecher Stowe, *Sunny Memories of Foreign Lands*, 2 vols. (Boston: Phillips, Sampson, 1854). *Uncle Tom's Cabin* began serially in 1851 in *National Era*, an American abolitionist newspaper. It was issued as a book in March 1852. Three hundred thousand copies were sold in the United States in the first ten months and one million in England. Within a year it had been translated into fifteen European languages. It was, of course, one of the greatest publishing bonanzas of all time, a fact that Brooks recognized.

74. William G. Brooks, Sr., Diary, 1858–61, 759, 793.

75. Ibid., 831.

76. William G. Brooks, Sr., Diary, 1863–66, 868.

77. See Brooks, *Joy of Preaching*, esp. chap. 3.

78. William G. Brooks, Sr., Diary, 1858–61, 652.

79. Ibid., 617. See also ibid., 614, 616, 619, 626, 633, 656; Mary Brooks to Phillips Brooks, 25 Mar. 1858, bMS AM 1594.1, (40), folder 1.

80. Phillips Brooks, Notebook, 1855–56, quoted in Allen, *Life and Letters*, 1:134.

81. William G. Brooks, Sr., Diary, 1853–57, 545. The date was 31 October 1856.

82. Mary Brooks to Phillips Brooks, 9 Oct. 1857, bMS AM 1594.1, (39), folder 1.

83. Mary Brooks to Phillips Brooks, 13 Nov. 1858, quoted in Allen, *Life and Letters*, 1:279.

84. William G. Brooks, Sr., to Phillips Brooks, 28 Jan. 1859, bMS AM 1594.1, (41), folder 1; William G. Brooks, Sr., to Phillips Brooks, 19 Mar. 1859, bMS AM1594.1, (41), folder 2.

85. Quoted in Allen, *Life and Letters*, 2:254.

Chapter 2: Growing Up in Boston's High Culture

1. Peter R. Knight, *The Plain People of Boston, 1830–1860: A Study in City Growth* (New York: Oxford University Press, 1971), 19–20. Dur-

ing this period of growth, Boston retained a compact, almost provincial quality; cities like New York, Philadelphia, and Baltimore were all larger. Even the rate of Boston's advance in population from 1830 to 1860 was not as great as that of other urban areas: 143 percent for the nation, 190 percent for Boston, but a whopping 464 percent for other major metropolitan centers (27–28). In the 1850s, the focus of this study, 61 percent of the city's inhabitants were born in New England (mostly in Massachusetts [50 percent]), and about 35 percent of the latter were native Bostonians; the other 39 percent were foreign-born, with 29 percent being Irish (34).

2. Robert Campbell, "Foreword," in Peter Vanderwarker, *Boston Then and Now* (New York: Dover, 1982), n.p.

3. Douglass Shand-Tucci, *Built in Boston: City and Suburb, 1800–1950* (Amherst: University of Massachusetts Press, 1988), 23.

4. Ibid., 35.

5. Kenneth Stampp, *America in 1857* (New York: Oxford University Press, 1990), 36–39. However, not everyone welcomed urbanization. In 1838, Ralph Waldo Emerson, possessor of "the imperial self," felt mean in the city's streets and wondered what would happen if someone accosted him on Washington Street (in downtown Boston); and then he worried whether he would be able to maintain his dignity if someone called him a "base fellow." Emerson wrote, "I should not be sure that I could make him feel by my answer & behaviour that my ends were worthy & noble." If the same thing should occur in the country, he went on, he felt he would acquit himself splendidly and "justify myself to his conscience." Presumably, if the accoster were a thief, it would not make that much difference if Emerson's ends were seen as worthy and noble or not, provided he had cash. Yet Emerson's fear was not so far off the mark. See William H. Gilman et al., eds., *The Journals and Miscellaneous Notebooks of Ralph Waldo Emerson*, vol. 7 (Cambridge: Harvard University Press, 1969), 158–59, quoted in John F. Kasson, *Rudeness and Civility: Manners in Nineteenth-Century Urban America* (New York: Hill and Wang, 1990), 113.

6. Arthur Mann, *Yankee Reformers in the Urban Age: Social Reform in Boston, 1880–1900* (New York: Belknap Press of Harvard University Press, 1966), 1–5.

7. Albright, *Focus*, 13.

8. For a brief history of early secondary education in Massachusetts, see Ronald D. Cohen, "Schools and Schooling," *Encyclopedia of the North American Colonies*, 3 vols. (New York: Charles Scribner's Sons, 1993) 3:461–74, esp. 462–63; and Pauline Holmes, *A Tercentenary History of the Boston Public Latin School, 1635–1935* (Cambridge: Harvard University Press, 1935), chap. 2.

E. Digby Baltzell writes, "For over 300 years the Latin School was the major preparatory school for Harvard College. As late as 1951, 102 of its graduates entered the freshman class at Harvard, far more than came from any one of the New England boarding schools" (*Puritan Boston and Quaker Philadelphia: Two Protestant Ethics and the Spirit of Class Authority and Leadership* [Boston: Beacon Press, 1979], 270). In 1925 the honor list of the admissions examination for Harvard contained eighty-two names, of which twenty-three were from the Boston Latin School. The nearest competitor was Exeter, with twenty-one, followed by Middlesex (five), Andover (four), English High (two), St. Mark's (one), Groton (one), St. Paul's (one), Milton (one), and Kent (one). The remaining twenty-two came from public high schools other than Boston Latin and English High; no other private schools had pupils on the list. See *Groton School Quarterly* 3, no. 7 (Mar. 1926), 152.

9. Theodore H. White, *In Search of History: A Personal Adventure* (New York: Harper and Row, 1978), 34.

10. Reprinted in Frank D. Ashburn, *Peabody of Groton: A Portrait* (New York: Coward McCann, 1944), 67.

11. White, *In Search of History.*

12. Others include Brooks's cousin Edward Everett; John Leverett, future governor of Massachusetts, who entered the school in 1635; William Stoughton, chief justice of the province of Massachusetts Bay; Charles Chauncy, liberal Congregationalist theologian; Thomas Hutchinson, last royal governor of Massachusetts; Samuel Adams, revolutionary patriot; Henry Knox, George Washington's artillery commander; Charles Bulfinch, architect; John Lothrop Motley, historian; Charles Sumner, antislavery senator from Massachusetts; John F. Fitzgerald, grandfather of President John F. Kennedy; Roy E. Larson, educator; and Arthur Fiedler, Boston Pops conductor.

13. Holmes, *Tercentenary History*, 275.

14. See, for instance, Howe, "Victorian Culture in America," 22.

15. These were only added gradually in the late 1860s and in the 1870s, but without giving up the classical curriculum.

16. Phillips Brooks, "Essay on the Articles of Religion," Miscellaneous Papers, bMS AM 1594.1, (635), box 19. Decius was consul in Rome, 340 B.C., in the Latin war, and, fulfilling a night vision, freely gave his life to assure a Roman victory. His son made the same sacrifice in 295 B.C. against the Gauls at the battle of Sentinum. His grandson was said to have followed suit in 279 B.C. against Pyrrhus, but the claim proved false as the young man survived.

17. Phillips Brooks, Notebook, 1849–50, bMS AM 1594.1, (635), box 19. Allen thinks the essay possesses "a deep self-revealing quality" (*Life and Letters*, 1:60).

18. Phillips Brooks to William G. Brooks, Jr., 25 Nov. 1859, bMS AM 1594.1, (6), folder 1.

19. C. A. L. Richards and the unnamed others are quoted in Allen, *Life and Letters*, 1:172; 2:19, 20, 772.

20. Albright, *Focus*, 19.

21. Phillips Brooks, "Unspotted from the World," *Sermons* (New York: E. P. Dutton, 1895), 174, 181.

22. Phillips Brooks, Notebook, 1857–58, bMS AM 1594.1, (635), box 23.

23. Phillips Brooks, "The Mystery of Iniquity," *Sermons: Sixth Series* (New York: E. P. Dutton, 1897), 11.

24. Brooks, "Unspotted from the World," 176.

25. Phillips Brooks, "The Priority of God," *The Light of the World and Other Sermons* (New York: E. P. Dutton, 1896), 54–55.

26. See Rose, *Victorian America*, 155–56. This view is probably exaggerated. No doubt Victorians sometimes innocently engaged in activities that to us would raise eyebrows. Joan D. Hedrick, in *Harriet Beecher Stowe: A Life* (New York: Oxford University Press, 1994), notes that Calvin Stowe, for solace at not being with Harriet, took another man to bed on more than one occasion (180–81)—and then wrote his wife of the incidents! It was not thought to be deviant behavior.

27. Brooks, *Joy of Preaching*, 147.

28. Sigmund Freud, "'Civilized' Sexual Morality and Modern Nervous Illness," *Standard Edition of the Complete Psychological Works,* trans. and ed. James Strachey et al., 24 vols. (London: Hogarth, 1953–74), 9:197.

29. Phillips Brooks, Notebook [A], 1858, bMS AM 1594.1, (635), box 19. (The notebook designations A, B, C are mine to distinguish the three journals for 1858.)

30. Hope to Woolverton, 10 Jan. 1994: "The growth spurt you describe is normal; presumably it coincided with pubertal development. The linear height certainly exceeded the mean of mid-nineteenth-century males, but there are always outliers on a normal distribution curve."

31. See, for instance, Phillips Brooks's sermon "The Law of Growth," in *The Law of Growth* (New York: E. P. Dutton, 1902), where he discerns nature as "the whole power of things immediately bearing him on" (12).

32. Brooks, *Joy of Preaching*, 88.

33. See Howe, "Victorian Culture in America," 4–5, 9.

34. See John F. Woolverton, "Stirring the Religious Pot at Harvard on the Eve of the Civil War: Two Huntingtons and a Cooke," *Anglican and Episcopal History* 58, no. 1 (Mar. 1989), 38. See also Lawrence A. Cremin, *American Education: The National Experience, 1783–1876*

(New York: Harper and Row, 1980), 405–6; and Seymour Martin Lipset and David Riesman, *Education and Politics at Harvard* (New York: McGraw-Hill, 1975), 82, 84.

35. Allen and, to a lesser degree, Albright try to make it out that Brooks "must" have been influenced one way or another by Theodore Parker, but there is no evidence of this. Allen claims that Brooks never heard of either Newman or Pusey, which seems unlikely. It would be more accurate to say that neither penetrated his thinking in the self-contained world of Harvard College. See Allen, *Life and Letters*, 1:87–88; see also Albright, *Focus*, 27, 32, 237.

36. Allen, *Life and Letters*, 1:79.

37. For comments on Chase, Sawyer, and Abbot, see Phillips Brooks, "Class of 1855," bMS AM 2022, (150). Information on Sawyer's career at the Utica Free Academy is courtesy of the Oneida County Historical Society. See also Daniel E. Wager, *Our County and Its People: A Descriptive Work on Oneida County* (Boston: Boston History Company, 1896), 346–52.

38. Allen, *Life and Letters*, 1:70–71.

39. It is perhaps significant that Brooks was not a member of the socially fashionable—and nationally representative—Porcellian Club. His friends and associates were middle-income students and more New England oriented.

40. For instance, following the publication of *Uncle Tom's Cabin,* when Stowe made her first triumphant tour of England in 1852, it was her husband, Calvin, who spoke on her behalf at the great abolitionist rally in Exeter Hall on May 16. See Stowe, *Sunny Memories,* 2:32–34.

41. Phillips Brooks, "The Lecturer," bMS AM 2022, (149), 3.

42. Phillips Brooks, "Manners as Related to Character," bMS AM 2022, (152), 12.

43. Ibid., 13, 14. I find no reference in the Phillips Brooks Papers to his having read *Uncle Tom's Cabin,* but by the summer of 1853 it seems unlikely, given the fame of the book and his own championing of blacks, that he would have failed to do so.

44. Phillips Brooks, "Man and His World," 27 Dec. 1853, bMS AM 2022, (153).

45. Ibid., 7.

46. Ibid., 11.

47. Ibid., 12.

48. Phillips Brooks, "The Huguenot Preacher," bMS AM 2022, (159), 3.

49. Ibid., 5.

50. On the side of Trinity Church that faces the John Hancock Building and the Copley Plaza Hotel, there is an unremarked statue of Brooks

above the porch. He is standing in a Rabautian manner, serenely looking down on the world of commerce and business. Though its placement is probably a coincidence, the statue is altogether fitting, far truer to Brooks's life and character than the presumptuous triumphalism of the St. Gaudens statue on the other side of the building.

51. Brooks, "Man and His World," 3.

52. Allen, *Life and Letters,* 2:601.

53. Morse Peckham, *The Triumph of Romanticism* (Columbia: University of South Carolina Press, 1970), 56. See also Roger Lundin, *The Culture of Interpretation: Christian Faith and the Postmodern World* (Grand Rapids, Mich.: William B. Eerdmans, 1993), 37–38.

54. Phillips Brooks, "The English Table-Talkers," bMS AM 1594.1, (635), box 19.

55. Something of the same attitude is conveyed in his essay "The Teaching of Tacitus Regarding Fate and Destiny" (bMS AM 2022, [162]), for which he won the Bowdoin Prize in his junior year. In it Brooks declares that Tacitus should have paid closer attention to Christianity, in which unlikely eventuality he would have been more hopeful to his contemporaries.

56. Phillips Brooks to William G. Brooks, Jr., 14 June 1855, bMS AM 1594.1, (2), "Letters [1855]." Phillips misspelled "crystallotype," a photographic picture on glass.

57. Phillips Brooks to William G. Brooks, Jr., 1 May 1859, bMS AM 1594.1, (41), "Letters 1859."

58. Phillips Brooks, "The Uses of Education: An Address at Brewster Academy," [1870s?], bMS AM 2022, (161), folder 1.

Chapter 3: Failure and the Poetry of Heroics

1. Ulrich Hoever, *Joseph Goebbels: Ein Nationaler Sozialist,* quoted in Gordon A. Craig, "The True Believer," *New York Review of Books* 41, no. 6 (Mar. 24, 1994), 7.

2. George B. Forgie, *Patricide in the House Divided: A Psychological Interpretation of Lincoln and His Age* (New York: W. W. Norton, 1979), 162, 160.

3. William G. Brooks, Sr., Diary, 1858–61, 795.

4. Stampp, *America in 1857,* 36–39.

5. James H. Moorhead, *American Apocalypse: Yankee Protestants and the Civil War, 1860–1869* (New Haven: Yale University Press, 1978), 91.

6. Phillips Brooks to William G. Brooks, Jr., 7 Nov. 1856, bMS AM 1594.1, (39), folder 2. Fillmore was the candidate of the Know-Nothing party in that election.

7. Phillips Brooks to William G. Brooks, Jr., 13 Jan. 1857, bMS AM 1594.1, (39), folder 1.

8. Karen Halttunen, *Confidence Men and Painted Women: A Study of Middle-Class Culture in America, 1830–1870* (New Haven: Yale University Press, 1982), 163.

9. Allen, *Life and Letters,* 2:767, 768, 765.

10. Halttunen, *Confidence Men,* 161. See also Allen, *Life and Letters,* 2:773, 769.

11. Kasson, *Rudeness and Civility,* 211.

12. Halttunen, *Confidence Men,* 165.

13. Allen, *Life and Letters,* 2:779–80, 768.

14. James F. White, *The Cambridge Movement: The Ecclesiologists and the Gothic Revival* (Cambridge: Cambridge University Press, 1962), chap. 8.

15. Walker Gwynne, *The Beginnings of Church Architecture in America* (New York, 1917), 3 (italics added).

16. Allen, *Life and Letters,* 2:765.

17. See Kasson, *Rudeness and Civility,* chaps. 6–7.

18. Halttunen, *Confidence Men,* 165.

19. Kasson, *Rudeness and Civility,* 157.

20. Allen, *Life and Letters,* 2:769.

21. Ibid.

22. For a discussion of the *Hierugia Anglicana,* see White, *Cambridge Movement,* 67.

23. Quoted in Alvin W. Skardon, *Church Leader in the Cities: William Augustus Muhlenberg* (Philadelphia: University of Pennsylvania Press, 1971), 189. See also ibid., chap. 8; John F. Woolverton, "William Augustus Muhlenberg and the Founding of St. Paul's College," *Historical Magazine of the Protestant Episcopal Church* 29, no. 3 (Sept. 1960), 200–201.

24. Donald M. Scott, *From Office to Profession: The New England Ministry, 1750–1850* (Philadelphia: University of Pennsylvania Press, 1978), 143.

25. Chorley, *Men and Movements,* chap. 13.

26. Allen, *Life and Letters,* 2:78.

27. Halttunen, *Confidence Men,* 188.

28. See Butler, "Standing against the Whirlwind," 261, 268–69, 286.

29. Ibid., 269, 275. The term "Tractarianism" refers to the teaching of those in England in the 1830s concerned with asserting the Church of England's independence from Parliament, the catholicity, and the spiritual authority of the church, especially that of bishops. The views of those in England who wrote *Tracts for the Times* deeply divided Episcopalians in America in the 1840s. See *Dictionary of Christianity in America,* s.v. "Tractarianism."

30. Butler, "Standing against the Whirlwind," 245.

31. George M. Fredrickson, *The Inner Civil War: Northern Intellectuals and the Crisis of the Union* (1965; Urbana: University of Illinois Press, 1993), 38.

32. Richard Rabinowitz, *The Spiritual Self in Everyday Life: The Transformation of Personal Religious Experience in Nineteenth-Century New England* (Boston: Northeastern University Press, 1989), 65.

33. Mullin, *Episcopal Vision/American Reality*, 178.

34. Rabinowitz, *Spiritual Self*, 238.

35. William G. Brooks, Jr., to Phillips Brooks, 7 Oct. 1856, bMS AM 2022, (9).

36. Allen attempts to make the case that Brooks went through a conversion experience (*Life and Letters*, 1:chap. 7); Albright wisely avoids making such a statement. Though there are comments on the general revival of 1857, I find no evidence in the Brooks Papers on such an occurrence in Brooks's life.

37. Charles Francis Adams, address at the Massachusetts Historical Society, 1893, quoted in Allen, *Life and Letters*, 1:102–5.

38. Albright, *Focus*, 28.

39. Phillips Brooks to George C. Sawyer, 20 Oct. 1855, quoted in Albright, *Focus*, 28. See also Phillips Brooks to George C. Sawyer, 1 Jan. 1856 and 14 Feb. 1856, quoted in ibid.

40. Brooks did, however, receive the Franklin Medal for excellence in Greek, Latin, and mathematics.

41. Sawyer taught for forty years at the Utica Academy. See Wager, *Our County and Its People*, 352.

42. Phillips Brooks to George C. Sawyer, 23 Sept. 1855, quoted in Allen, *Life and Letters*, 1:113.

43. Phillips Brooks to George C. Sawyer, 9 Dec. 1855, quoted in Allen, *Life and Letters*, 1:115.

44. Phillips Brooks to George C. Sawyer, 19 Jan. 1856, quoted in Allen, *Life and Letters*, 1:115.

45. Adams, 1893 address, quoted in Allen, *Life and Letters*, 1:105.

46. Phillips Brooks, Notebook [A], 1858, bMS AM 1594.1, (635), box 23.

47. For a psychological description of this maturing process, see Erik H. Erikson, "The Growth and Crises of the Healthy Personality," *Psychological Issues* 1, no. 1 (1959), 50–100, esp. 88–99.

48. Phillips Brooks, "Leaves from a journal . . . ," Feb. 1856–Oct. 1856, bMS AM 1594.1, (635).

49. William G. Brooks, Sr., Diary 1853–57, 521.

50. Phillips Brooks to George C. Sawyer, 2 July 1856, quoted in Allen, *Life and Letters*, 1:119.

51. Halttunen, *Confidence Men,* 59.

52. Allen, *Life and Letters,* 1:121.

53. Phillips Brooks to George C. Sawyer, 5 Mar. 1856, quoted in Allen, *Life and Letters,* 1:118.

54. Phillips Brooks to George C. Sawyer, [?] June 1856, quoted in Allen, *Life and Letters,* 1:118–19.

55. Phillips Brooks to George C. Sawyer, 2 July 1856, quoted in Allen, *Life and Letters,* 1:119.

56. Brooks, "Leaves from a journal . . . ," 8. Shelley was actually nineteen at the time.

57. George Steiner, *Real Presences* (Chicago: University of Chicago Press, 1989), 177.

58. Brooks, "Leaves from a journal . . . ," 8.

59. Ibid.

60. Ibid.

61. Harold Bloom, "The Unpastured Sea: An Introduction to Shelley," *Romanticism and Consciousness: Essays in Criticism,* ed. Harold Bloom (New York: W. W. Norton, 1970), 386.

62. George Henry Lewes, *The Life of Goethe,* 2 vols. (London: G. Routledge, 1855).

63. Phillips Brooks, Notebook [C], 1858, bMS AM 2022, (26), 34.

64. Ibid. There was nothing particularly new in Americans' fascination with either Goethe or Shelley. See Drew Gilpin Faust, *A Sacred Circle: The Dilemma of the Intellectual in the Old South, 1840–1860* (Baltimore: Johns Hopkins University Press, 1977), 19–24.

65. Steiner, *Real Presences,* 188–89.

66. See Allen, *Life and Letters,* 1:227. For Coleridge's influence via James Marsh, see Ronald V. Wells, *Three Christian Transcendentalists* (New York: Columbia University Press, 1943). To my knowledge Wells was one of the first to point out the significance of Marsh. Not all Romantics found Coleridge convincing; John Ruskin was closer to William Paley and saw God mirrored in nature without benefit of Coleridge's "subjectivism." See Graham Hough, *The Last Romantics* (London: Methuen, 1947), 31–32.

67. Bruce Kucklick, *Churchmen and Philosophers: From Jonathan Edwards to John Dewey* (New Haven: Yale University Press, 1985), 122.

68. Ibid.

69. Samuel Taylor Coleridge, *Aids to Reflection* (New York: F. Warne, 1905), 145, 196–202.

70. For further discussion, see J. Robert Barth, S.J., *Coleridge and Christian Doctrine* (Cambridge: Harvard University Press, 1969), 20. See also M. H. Abrams, "Structure and Style in the Greater Romantic Lyric," in *Romanticism and Consciousness,* ed. Bloom, 218.

71. Philip F. Gura, *The Wisdom of Words: Language, Theology, and Literature in the New England Renaissance* (Middletown: Wesleyan University Press, 1981), 39.

72. Brooks, "Poetry," *Essays and Addresses,* 236, 234–35.

73. Ibid., 237, 238.

74. Ibid., 238, 239, 241. Throughout Brooks's essay there are obvious parallels with Emerson's "The Poet," and it seems likely that the latter served as a model for Brooks, especially in his emphasis on aesthetics. While Emerson rejoiced in the birth of the poet in his own time, Brooks tended to show how that birth happened and to analyze it. See Ralph Waldo Emerson, "The Poet," *Essays: First and Second Series* (Mount Vernon, N.Y.: Peter Pauper Press, n.d.), 191. For further discussion of the role of the poet in Emerson's thought, see Lundin, *Culture of Interpretation,* 70–72.

75. Brooks, "Poetry," 242, 243.

76. Ibid., 245–46.

77. Quoted in M. H. Abrams, *The Mirror and the Lamp: Romantic Theory and the Critical Tradition* (London: Oxford University Press, 1953), 48.

78. Albright, *Focus,* 180–81, wonders whether Henry Adams's *Esther: A Novel* is not an account of a failed love affair involving a thinly disguised Brooks—Stephen Hazard—and a woman. Albright goes on to ask whether Brooks was in love during the period that is described in *Esther* of the building and decorating of Trinity Church. "The answer is clear and definitely in the affirmative," judges Albright, who further suggests that the woman was Sara Gemma Timmins, who is portrayed in the heroine of the novel. The evidence of a love affair between Brooks and Timmins appears flimsy, given that his expressions of regret at her early death are altogether perfunctory. See Phillips Brooks to Mrs. Henry Whitman, 19 June 1890, quoted in Albright, *Focus,* 183.

79. Phillips Brooks to William G. Brooks, Jr., 13 Jan. 1857, quoted in Albright, *Focus,* 39.

80. Phillips Brooks to William G. Brooks, Jr., 20 Nov. 1857, quoted in Allen, *Life and Letters,* 1:200.

81. Brooks, untitled poem [1], Notebook [A], 1858, bMS AM 1594.1, (635), box 19, 206.

82. Ibid., 222.

83. Brooks, untitled poem [2], Notebook [A], 1858, bMS AM 1594.1, (635), box 19, 62–63.

84. Donald Yacavone, "Abolitionists and the 'Language of Fraternal Love'," in *Meanings for Manhood,* ed. Carnes and Griffen, 86. William S. McFeely suggests that before Freud taught us to "leap at every signal" and before the word "homosexuality" became common, a man could

write openly about male friendship without "betraying even a hint of any sexual activity that might have been a component of that friendship" (*Frederick Douglass* [New York: W. W. Norton, 1991], 66).

85. See R. H. A. Jenkyns, *The Victorians and Ancient Greece* (Oxford: Basil Blackwell, 1980). Robert Bernard Martin, *With Friends Possessed: A Life of Edward Fitzgerald* (New York: Atheneum, 1985), 117, calls it "perilous" for twentieth-century males to describe their friendships in similar fashion.

86. Donald Yacavone, "'Surpassing the Love of Women': Fraternal Love in Anglo-America," paper delivered at the 1992 Organization of American Historians conference, 2.

87. See Thomas E. Jeffrey, "'Our Remarkable Friendship': The Secret Collaboration of Calvin H. Wiley and John W. Cunningham," *North Carolina Historical Review* 67, no. 1 (Jan. 1990), 57, with reference to Carroll Smith-Rosenberg, "The Female World of Love and Ritual: Relations between Women in Nineteenth-Century America," *Signs* 1 (Autumn 1975), 1–29.

88. Martin, *With Friends Possessed,* 118. See also Peter Gay, *The Tender Passion: The Bourgeois Experience, Victoria to Freud* (New York: Oxford University Press, 1986), 206–12, for a description of the diary of Albert Dodd.

89. Yacavone, "'Surpassing the Love of Women.'" See also Joanne P. Zuckerman, "Tennyson's 'In Memoriam' as Love Poetry," *Dalhousie Review* 51 (Summer 1971), 202.

90. Lewis Mumford, *The Brown Decades: A Study of the Arts in America, 1865–1895* (1931; New York: Dover, 1971), 2.

91. As Erikson has remarked about the lack in some of the desire to produce and care for the offspring of one's union with one's mate, "there are people who, from misfortune or because of special and genuine gifts in other directions, do not apply this drive to offspring but to other forms of altruistic concern and of creativity which may absorb their kind of parental responsibility" (*The Healthy Personality,* 97). Brooks may have been such a man.

92. Howe, "The Victorian Crisis of Faith," in *Victorian America,* ed. Howe, 17.

93. Phillips Brooks, "The Sea of Glass Mingled with Fire," *Twenty Sermons* (New York: E. P. Dutton, 1895), 119.

94. Robert Browning, "Bishop Blougram's Apology," *Poetic and Dramatic Works of Robert Browning,* 6 vols. (Boston: Houghton, Mifflin, 1899), 4:96. I am indebted to Bayard Clark, a Brooks collector and scholar, for drawing my attention to the influence on Brooks of this poem by Browning.

95. Ibid.
96. Allen, *Life and Letters*, 1:121.
97. Quoted in ibid., 1:122.
98. Lundin, *Culture of Interpretation*, 58.

Chapter 4: Virginia Seminary

1. Popular today in church circles among the followers of C. G. Jung, this type of thinking remakes biblical histories and their particularities into images or metaphors illustrative of one or more aspects of general human experience. See Phillip J. Lee, *Against the Protestant Gnostics* (New York: Oxford University Press, 1987), esp. chap. 10.

2. W. A. R. Goodwin, *History of the Theological Seminary in Virginia*, 2 vols. (New York: Edwin S. Gorham, 1923), 1:160, 2:72.

3. Phillips Brooks to William G. Brooks, Jr., 7 Nov. 1856, bMS AM 1594.1, (39), folder 3.

4. Ibid.

5. Phillips Brooks to William G. Brooks, Sr., 18 Dec. 1857, bMS AM 1594.1, (39), folder 3.

6. Phillips Brooks to William G. Brooks, Sr., 1 Oct. 1858, bMS AM 1594.1, (5), folder 2.

7. Phillips Brooks to George Brooks, 23 Dec. 1857, bMS AM 2022, (26).

8. Phillips Brooks to William G. Brooks, Sr., 17 Dec. 1857, bMS AM 1594.1, (3), folder 2.

9. William G. Brooks, Sr., to Phillips Brooks, 21 Dec. 1857, bMS AM 1594.1, (41).

10. Mary Brooks to Phillips Brooks, 26 May 1859, bMS AM 1594.1, (41).

11. McPherson, *Battle Cry of Freedom*, 35.

12. William G. Brooks, Sr., to Phillips Brooks, 31 May 1859, bMS AM 1594.1, (41). On Wendell Phillips, see Lewis Perry, *Radical Abolitionism: Anarchy and the Government of God in Antislavery Thought* (Ithaca: Cornell University Press, 1973), 161–66. For Episcopalians and abolitionism, see Mullin, *Episcopal Vision/American Reality*, 206–11. See also John R. McKivigan, *The War against Proslavery Religion: Abolitionism and the Northern Churches, 1830–1865* (Ithaca: Cornell University Press, 1984), 50, 95, 190.

13. Phillips Brooks to Frederick Brooks, 7 Feb. 1859, bMS AM 1594.1, (6), trans. James Mulvey. Charles Parker, associate professor of classics at Harvard in the 1890s, in a letter to Alexander V. G. Allen, declared that Brooks's Latin letter to Frederick was "full of life, and the

passage about slavery has an intrinsic interest." Parker continued: "In my opinion Phillips Brooks should not have wished the publication of it. . . . all things considered I must doubt the advisability of printing any of it" (Parker to Allen, 20 Jan. 1896, bMS AM 1594.2, [48]). No doubt intrinsic interest collided with the interests of Harvard College or of the Episcopal church, or perhaps of both.

14. Allen, *Life and Letters*, 1:463–64, 520.

15. Phillips Brooks to William G. Brooks, Jr., 20 Nov. 1857, quoted in Allen, *Life and Letters*, 1:201.

16. Sumner of Massachusetts was the foremost exponent in the Senate of the abolition of slavery. Two days before this incident he made a speech attacking the absent Senator Andrew P. Butler of South Carolina, who was a relative of Preston Brooks. So severely was Sumner beaten that he was unable to return to the Senate for three years. See Frederick J. Blue, *Charles Sumner and the Conscience of the North* (Arlington Heights, Ill.: Harlan Davidson, 1994), 93–99.

17. Phillips Brooks to William G. Brooks, Jr., 20 Nov. 1857, quoted in Allen, *Life and Letters,* 1:201.

18. Phillips Brooks to George Brooks, [?] Mar. 1858, bMS AM 2022, (26).

19. McPherson, *Battle Cry of Freedom,* 198.

20. Phillips Brooks to William G. Brooks, Jr., 7 Nov. 1856, bMS AM 1594.1, (3). Massachusetts was safely in the Frémont column in the presidential election of that year. Brooks's allegiance to the Frémont ticket, however, appears unusual for an Episcopalian. Most of Frémont's support in the state came from Congregationalists and Unitarians, with an increasing number of Methodists and Baptists joining the Republican party. See William E. Gienapp, *The Origins of the Republican Party, 1852–1856* (New York: Oxford University Press, 1987), 433–34.

21. Stampp, *America in 1857,* 36.

22. Phillips Brooks to "Top" [Sawyer], 8 Feb. 1857, bMS AM 1594.1, (4), folder 3.

23. See *Catalogue of the Theological Seminary in Virginia, 1858–1859* (Fairfax County, Va., 1859).

24. Brooks, *Joy of Preaching,* 50–51.

25. Quoted in Allen, *Life and Letters,* 1:256.

26. Phillips Brooks to George C. Sawyer, 14 Nov. 1856, quoted in Albright, *Focus,* 35.

27. Phillips Brooks to William G. Brooks, Sr., 16 Mar. 1857, bMS AM 1594.1, (4), folder 3. For the number of books in the seminary's library, see Joseph Packard, *Recollections of a Long Life* (Washington, D.C.: Byron S. Adams, 1902), 305.

28. Phillips Brooks to William G. Brooks, Sr., 8 May 1857, bMS AM 1594.1, (4), folder 1. See also Phillips Brooks to William G. Brooks, Jr., 1 June 1857, and Phillips Brooks to George Brooks, 9 Sept. 1857, both in bMS AM 1594.1, (4), folder 2. The judgment on Packard is harsh; his usefulness is attested perhaps by the fact that he taught at Virginia Theological Seminary until 1902.

29. Packard, *Recollections,* 301. Stuart judged that Packard had made "unusual progress in the Greek and Hebrew Scriptures" (68). By Packard's own admission, and despite his efforts to commend education in the Old Dominion, the Virginia seminary was, as he said, "not the ideal theological school of to-day; no less backward were the law and medical schools" of Virginia (*Recollections,* 304). The professor had every reason to speak well of southern institutions—and generally did—for he had married into the Lee family and saw his sons do service in the Confederate army.

30. Phillips Brooks to William G. Brooks, Sr., 8 May 1857, bMS AM 1594.1, (4), folder 1. While word on the relative merits of theological schools in antebellum America awaits more complete treatment, Andover would indeed appear to represent the best of its kind in the land (see Cremin, *American Education,* 360–63). It was followed by Princeton Seminary, Mercersburg, Yale University's Department of Theology, and Gettysburg, for the Lutherans (see Glenn Miller and Robert Lynn, "Christian Theological Education," *Encyclopedia of American Religion,* 3:1630–38). Union Theological Seminary in New York City had not yet reached a prominence it held for nearly three quarters of a century, from the 1890s onward. "On the Education of Ministers," Charles W. Eliot's challenge to the Harvard Divinity School, did not appear before 1883—to be repeated in kind, if not word-for-word, by two twentieth-century presidents of Harvard, Nathan M. Pusey and Derek Bok (see Cremin, *American Education,* 496).

31. See Robert W. Prichard, "Nineteenth-Century Episcopal Attitudes on Predestination and Election," *Historical Magazine of the Protestant Episcopal Church* 51, no. 1 (Mar. 1982), 40.

32. Phillips Brooks to William G. Brooks, Sr., 21 June 1857, bMS AM 1594.1, (4), folder 2. After the Philadelphia Divinity School opened its doors in 1861, it earned an enviable reputation for academic excellence. Brooks himself was involved in its affairs from 1859 to 1869 and, in 1864, was invited by its trustees to become professor of church history.

33. Ibid.

34. Phillips Brooks, untitled paper on Origen in packet labeled "P.B.," bMS AM 1594.1, (635), box 19. Brooks also mentions Origen's "youthful sacrifice" (of castration).

35. Phillips Brooks to William G. Brooks, Sr., 8 Feb. 1857, bMS AM 1594.1, (4), folder 1.

36. Phillips Brooks, "The Style of New Testament Greek," bMS AM 1594.1, (635), box 19. It only half dawned on Brooks that there might be power, beauty, and a stylistic meaning beyond "smoothness" in the language of Mark's Gospel. See Auerbach, *Mimesis*, 40–49.

37. Phillips Brooks to William G. Brooks, Sr., 1 June 1857, bMS AM 1594.1, (4), folder 2.

38. Phillips Brooks to William G. Brooks, Sr., 8 May 1857, bMS AM 1594.1, (4), folder 2.

39. See Cornelius Walker, *The Life and Correspondence of Rev. William Sparrow* (Philadelphia: James Hammond, 1876), 17–52.

40. See Goodwin, *History of the Theological Seminary*, 1:188.

41. J. Barrett Miller, "The Theology of William Sparrow," *Historical Magazine of the Protestant Episcopal Church* 46, no. 4 (Dec. 1977), 450, 449.

42. Goodwin, *History of the Theological Seminary*, 1:613. See also Chorley, *Men and Movements*, 79.

43. Butler, "Standing against the Whirlwind," 63. Evangelical Episcopalians believed first in ecclesiastical election and then in that of the individual because God had elected the whole church. This election was not tied to any particular view of divine foreknowledge or free will.

44. Miller, "Theology of William Sparrow," 446 and passim. On human depravity, see Walker, *Life and Correspondence*, 234.

45. Alexander C. Zabriskie, "The Rise and Major Characteristics of the Anglican Evangelical Movement in England and America," in *Anglican Evangelicalism*, ed. A. C. Zabriskie (Philadelphia: Church Historical Society, 1943), 27. Prichard, "Episcopal Attitudes," notes that Sparrow held these views in common with John S. Stone, the rector of St. Paul's Church, who was in the early years the Brookses' pastor and theologian (39).

46. William Sparrow to E. W. Syle, 6 Oct. 1854, in Walker, *Life and Correspondence*, 224.

47. William Sparrow to [?], 20 Apr. 1857, in Walker, *Life and Correspondence*, 233.

48. William Sparrow to [?], 18 Nov. 1854, in Walker, *Life and Correspondence*, 223.

49. Phillips Brooks, Notebook, 1849–50, bMS AM 1594.1, (635), box 19. None of Brooks's biographers mention this essay, which anticipates his later interests.

50. George Christian Knapp, *Lectures on Christian Theology*, 2 vols. (New York: G. and C. and H. Carvill, 1831). Pietists were late seventeenth-

century western Christians who reasserted the experiential tradition in postreformation Protestantism. They demanded that one discern a special spiritual sense of Scripture above the ordinary grammatical and logical sense. They emphasized certain sacred words beyond the meaning those words have in ordinary usage. At the same time pietists had a passion for finding the same saving truth in all the biblical texts. Their purpose was to enhance a meaningful relationship of the individual with God. "Personal" repentance and faith, assurance of membership in God's kingdom, warm devotion, and lively preaching for conversion marked the movement in Germany, England, and America in the eighteenth century.

51. Ibid., 1:x. I find no evidence to support Allen's claim that F. D. Maurice's *Theological Essays* were read by Brooks during his formative years in theological school, much less influenced him later in his career. In this case the wish is father to the fact. See Allen, *Life and Letters,* 1:228, 229.

52. Knapp, *Lectures,* 1:viii.

53. See T. H. L. Parker, "A Comparison of Calvin and Luther on Galatians," *Interpretation* 17 (1963), 61–75.

54. Packard, *Recollections,* 171. See also Allen, *Life and Letters,* 1:310.

55. Knapp, *Lectures,* 2:291, 318, 319, 372.

56. Packard, *Recollections,* 171–72.

57. Brooks, "Essay on the Articles of Religion." Note that Brooks had been reading Ernst Wilhelm Hengstenberg's *Christology of the Old Testament,* published in English in 1854 and used at the seminary. Hengstenberg traced the "Messianic prophesies" in their "historical order and connection" (x). Without doubt this was an important volume in Brooks's theological development.

58. Phillips Brooks, "Notes for a Paper on Christology," Miscellaneous Papers, bMS AM 1594.1, (635), box 19.

59. Ibid.

60. Ibid.

61. Phillips Brooks, Notebook [B], 1858, bMs AM 1594.1, (635), box 19, 69.

62. Ibid., 130.

Chapter 5: The Search for the Ideal

1. Among the more famous were Francis Hutcheson, Thomas Reid, Dugald Stewart, and Adam Ferguson. Common Sense philosophers were followers of the inductive method of reasoning of Francis Bacon. They criticized John Locke's notion of the mind as a tabula rasa and were fear-

ful of George Berkeley's and Jonathan Edwards's idealism, as well as of David Hume's skepticism; they claimed that the mind's operations are innate and that a person's "common sense" includes the ability to discern moral norms and make moral judgments. While they acknowledged God's controlling power, they were more intent on establishing in humankind semi-independent grounds for discriminating right from wrong. For his part, Edwards drew a sharp distinction between one who knows that there is such a thing as right—or in his case beauty—and one who has experienced the right in the glorious harmony and excellence of divine things. Edwards began not with humankind's natural sense of moral responsibility but with God, who was the origin of all benevolence and virtue.

2. Francis Wayland, *The Elements of Moral Science* (Boston: Gould and Lincoln, 1855), 46.

3. Ibid., 50 (see also 36), 118–19, 125, 142. Wayland also wrote: "Natural religion presents us with more distinct and affecting views of the character of God than could be obtained without it. One of the first aspirations of a human soul is after an Intelligent First Cause" (127).

4. E. W. Syle, "Reminiscences of Dr. Sparrow," in Walker, *Life and Correspondence*, 391, 392.

5. Kucklick, *Churchmen and Philosophers*, 130–31.

6. Plato and Aristotle were of course not far apart at all in their ethics, despite Aristotle's attack on his teacher. Differences between the two nearly vanish when they are subjected to examination. However, Plato made no serious attempt to deduce the particulars of human well-being from his knowledge of the absolute good. For his part, Aristotle discarded Plato's transcendentalism but retained the Socratic method of induction from and verification by common opinion. Popularly, the difference is more marked and revolves around the question of who is to occupy the foreground, so to say, humankind or God. A continuously creating God (à la Edwards) willy-nilly takes center stage; a First Cause "prompts" but remains offstage, leaving us to act out the scene.

7. From Brooks's poem "Back Once Again," Notebook [B], 1858, bMS AM 1594.2, (78). See also "What Memories of the Town Remain?" Notebook [B], 1858, bMS AM 1594.2, (78), 40, where Brooks speaks of "A moment's good not half received / A moment's truth not half believed, / A moment's glimpse of moon and sun." Yet the central figure in this poem had "A little gleam of God's great grace, / . . . [and so] We hurried onward in our race, / To see our Maker's living face." Compare Brooks here with Tennyson, *In Memoriam*, 8, stanza 4: "I falter where I firmly trod, / And falling with my weight of cares / Upon the world's great altar-stairs / That slope thro' darkness up to God."

8. In classical Anglicanism Christians are justified by the righteousness of Christ *imputed* to them and not by any inherent righteousness of their own. The inherent righteousness of sanctification is the growth in Christians of grateful response to what Christ has done.

9. Brooks, *Essays and Addresses,* 1.

10. Phillips Brooks, Notebook [C], 1858, bMS AM 1594.2, (78).

11. Phillips Brooks, "Of the Decade of the 1640s in England," Miscellaneous Papers, bMS AM 1594.1, (635), box 19. A strikingly different Episcopalian view was expressed by Brooks's contemporary Peter Oliver in *The Puritan Commonwealth* (Boston: Little Brown, 1856). While it seems likely that Brooks would have known of this able and polemical work against the Puritans, I have found no evidence of such knowledge in his papers.

12. Brooks, "Of the Decade of the 1640s in England."

13. See David Harlan, "A People Blind from Birth: American History according to Sacvan Berkovitch," *Journal of American History* 78, no. 3 (Dec. 1991), passim.

14. Phillips Brooks, "Two Hundred and Seventy-second Anniversary of the Landing of the Pilgrims," *Essays and Addresses,* 513.

15. Hans W. Frei, *The Eclipse of the Biblical Narrative: A Study in Eighteenth- and Nineteenth-Century Hermeneutics* (New Haven: Yale University Press, 1974), 49. Blacks in the antebellum South possessed the same precritical view of the Bible and their identity as mediated to them through it. See Henry H. Mitchell, *Black Preaching* (Philadelphia: Lippincott, 1970), 49–50, 101, 112–13, 133; and Eugene D. Genovese, *Roll, Jordan, Roll: The World the Slaves Made* (New York: Pantheon, 1972), 232–79.

16. Abrams, *The Mirror and the Lamp,* 22.

17. Ibid., 59–60.

18. Brooks, "Landing of the Pilgrims," 518 (italics added).

19. Ibid., 512. On George Bancroft see Jan C. Dawson, *The Usable Past* (Chico, Calif.: Scholar's Press, 1984), 11–12; for a broader perspective, see 22–38.

20. See, for instance, Richard L. Greaves, "Radicals, Rights, and Revolution: British Nonconformity and the Roots of the American Experience," *Church History* 61, no. 2 (June 1992), 151–68, esp. 155.

21. Brooks, "Landing of the Pilgrims," 518.

22. Phillips Brooks to Arthur Brooks, 21 Dec. 1885, quoted in Albright, *Focus,* 209.

23. Charles L. Cohen, "Puritanism," *Encyclopedia of the North American Colonies,* 3:590.

24. Lawrence Buell, *New England Literary Culture: From Revolution*

through Renaissance (Cambridge: Cambridge University Press, 1989), 239–80, quotations on 246, 268, 262.

25. Brooks showed traces of Hawthorne's influence, however. When he spoke specifically of *The Scarlet Letter,* he noted its "grimness" and thus its otherness from the nineteenth century. See "The Boston Latin School," *Essays and Addresses,* 404–5.

26. Contemporary Puritan studies have shown that the American Puritan movement was not a monolithic unity, that conversion was not a one-time affair, and that Puritanism in New England was not so exceptional and set apart from the English tradition, as had been thought in the 1940s and 1950s. Locating American Puritanism within the reform tradition generally makes Brooks's adherence to it, while still an Anglican, less a matter of profound difference and exception within his own church. For a review of Puritan studies to 1987, see David D. Hall, "On Common Ground: The Coherence of American Puritan Studies," *William and Mary Quarterly* (3d ser.) 44, no. 2 (June 1987), passim.

27. Dawson, *The Usable Past,* 43.

28. Brooks, *The Candle of the Lord,* 7. The sermon was preached on 4 July 1880 at Westminster Abbey in London.

29. For a discussion of such typology, see Sacvan Bercovitch, *The Puritan Origins of the American Self* (New Haven: Yale University Press, 1975), 35–48 and passim.

30. See, for example, Thomas Hooker, "The Activity of Faith or Abraham's Imitators," in Ahlstrom, *Theology in America,* 114–48.

31. Sparrow had first-year students read Butler's *Analogy,* but I have been unable to discover any evidence that Hooker's *Laws* was read by anyone in the class. See Goodwin, *History of the Theological Seminary,* 1:191.

32. Karl Barth, *Church Dogmatics,* trans. and ed. G. W. Bromiley and T. F. Torrance, 14 vols. (Edinburgh: T. and T. Clark, 1956–80), IV, 1, 522. Brooks and Kähler were born in the same year, 1835. See also Carl Braaten, "Introduction," in Martin Kähler, *The So-called Historical Jesus and the Historical Biblical Christ,* trans. and ed. Carl Braaten (Philadelphia: Fortress Press, 1964), 8.

33. Martin Kähler, *Die Wissenchaft der christlichen Lehre, von dem evangelischen Grundartikel aus in Abriss dargestellt* (Leipzig: A. Deichert, 1883, 1893, 1905).

34. See John H. Rodgers, *The Theology of P. T. Forsyth* (London: Independent Press, 1965), 16.

35. Ronald Story, *Harvard and the Boston Upper Class: Forging an Aristocracy, 1800–1870* (Middletown: Wesleyan University Press, 1980), 124–26.

36. Phillips Brooks, Notebook [B], 1858, bMS AM 1594.1, 141. Again

and again in this notebook Brooks cites Tertulllian's work: *Apologia, De Idolatria, De Praescriptione Haereticorum, De Carne Christi, De Corona Militis, De Fuga in Persecutione, De Testimonia Anima,* and the *De Resurrectionis.*

37. The last clause of Brook's statement reminds the reader of Friedrich Schleiermacher's "consciousness of being absolutely dependent" (*The Christian Faith* [Philadelphia: Fortress Press, 1976], 12–13.

38. Brooks, untitled paper on Origen.

39. Allen, *Life and Letters,* 1:228. This claim may be overstated.

40. Brooks's use of the imagery of the sun and of light would seem to have been derived from the line of march that went from Philo to Clement to Augustine, but also, I think, from Tertullian. For a discussion of this subject see Jaroslav Pelikan, *Light of the World* (New York: Harper Brothers, 1960), 12 and passim, where the author draws attention to the pioneering work of Franz Joseph Dolger on the relation of Christianity to its Philonic milieu.

41. Phillips Brooks, notes entitled "Faith and Life," Notebook, 1879, bMS AM 1594.2, (58).

42. Heinrich Ewald's *Die Lehre der Bibel von Gott oder Theologie des Alten und Neuen Bundes* dominated Old Testament studies during the 1870s and even later. A major change in historical, critical studies came about with the publication of Julius Wellhausen's *Prolegomena zur Geschichte Israels* (1878). Wellhausen was an Orientalist and founder of the history of religion school of Old Testament studies. Karl Theodor Keim was a lecturer in New Testament and church history at Tübingen University. His monumental work in three volumes was entitled *Die Geschichte Jesu von Nazara in ihrer Verkettung mit dem Gemsamtleben seines Volkes.* Emil Shuerer, another German Protestant theologian and friend of Adolph Harnack, is the author of *Lehrbuch der neutestamentlichen Zeitgeschichte* (1874). Brooks generally spoke in favor of freedom of examination of Scripture (e.g., "Authority and Conscience," *Essays and Addresses,* 113–14).

43. Richard N. Bolles, "Phillips Brooks: Apostle of Comprehensiveness" (Ms., St. Mark's Library, General Theological Seminary, New York), 47.

44. Steiner, *Real Presences,* 38.

45. Ibid., 39.

46. Phillips Brooks, "Centralizing Power of the Gospel," *Essays and Addresses,* 3.

47. Ibid., 4.

48. Hans W. Frei, *Types of Christian Theology* (New Haven: Yale University Press, 1992), 29, 21.

49. Brooks, "Centralizing Power of the Gospel," 5.

50. Phillips Brooks, "The Opening of the Eyes," *Light of the World,* 202.

51. Phillips Brooks, *Lectures on Preaching* (New York: E. P. Dutton, 1893), 47.

52. Phillips Brooks, "The Style of N.T. Greek," Miscellaneous Papers, bMS AM 1594.1, (635), box 19, 6.

53. Phillips Brooks, Notebook, 1879, bMS AM 1594.2, (58), 1A. See, for instance, Tertullian, *Adversus Praxeas,* V, VIII, XIV.

54. For the sake of readability, I have kept Brooks's citations of texts to a minimum; suffice it to say, he listed many New Testament sources for each of his claims.

55. Phillips Brooks, "Faith and Morals," Notebook, 1879, bMS AM 1594.2, (58), 12. Unlike Marlow, Lessing proclaimed that the ultimate end of Faust must not be his damnation but his salvation. Goethe picked up on this change and introduced it into his own *Faust,* but the idea was Lessing's. We have only the "fragment" of Lessing's story of which Brooks spoke; the rest of it was lost sometime around 1770.

56. Phillips Brooks, "Faith and Pleasure," Notebook, 1879, bMS AM 1594.2, (58), 13.

57. Jonathan Edwards, "The Distinguishing Mark of a Work of the Spirit of God," *The Great Awakening,* ed. C. C. Goen (New Haven: Yale University Press, 1972), 281–82.

58. Quoted in Allen, *Life and Letters,* 2:735.

59. Jonathan Edwards, "Miscellanies," *The Philosophy of Jonathan Edwards from His Private Notebooks,* ed. Harvey G. Townsend (Eugene: University of Oregon Press, 1955), 189.

60. Quoted in Allen, *Life and Letters,* 2:349.

61. Ibid., 349–50.

62. Phillips Brooks, "Faith and Society," Notebook, 1879, bMS AM 1594.2, (58), 3. See Matthew 11:18 and Luke 7:34. See also Hans W. Frei, "The Encounter of Jesus with the German Academy," *Types of Christian Theology,* 133–46, esp. 136–37.

63. In the Notebook, 1879, Brooks uses this term without biblical citation. However, in *The Influence of Jesus* (New York: E. P. Dutton, 1879), he carefully spells out those rights—and does so repeatedly—using the following passages: John 8:1–11 (36–38, 120–22); Mark 14:3–9 (38–40, 92–93); John 11:1–44 (93–94); Mark 5:21–43 (165); John 19:25–27 (180–82); Matthew 15:21–28 (197). Since Brooks worked from the Notebook when he wrote what was eventually published as *The Influence of Jesus,* we can safely surmise that he knew these passages so well that he did not need to remind himself of their location in the New

Testament. What is curious with respect to his awareness of "women's rights" is that he did not refer to Luke 10:38–42.

64. Brooks, Notebook, 1879, bMS AM 1594.2, (58), 2.

65. Ibid., 37, 56.

66. Phillips Brooks, Sermon 286, 26 Oct. 1861, Trinity Church Archives at the New England Historic Genealogical Society, box 1, file 5.

67. See Clebsch in *American Religious Thought:* "The world Emerson occupied was less an ethical than an esthetic universe . . . available to the new religious sense in every experience of being at home with nature, humanity, and divinity" (105). However, he fails to state that Emerson recklessly abandoned the indivisibility between matter and form in art and thus had little to say about the autonomous integrity and internality of particular works of art. As Emerson declared, "nothing is so fleeting as form," that is, the incarnation of reason (logos). It was a view to which neither Edwards nor Brooks could possibly subscribe. F. O. Mathiessen acidly noted that Emerson's "religious veneration of genius led him into scorn of talent as trivial impertinence" (*American Renaissance* [London: Oxford University Press, 1941], 26).

68. Phillips Brooks, "The Manliness of Jesus," *The Candle of the Lord,* 261. See also Roland Delattre, *Beauty and Sensibility in the Thought of Jonathan Edwards: An Essay in Aesthetics and Theological Ethics* (New Haven: Yale University Press, 1968), 15–26, 191–96.

69. Phillips Brooks, "Biography," *Essays and Addresses,* 448.

70. Frei, *Types of Christian Theology,* 11.

71. Phillips Brooks, *The Influence of Jesus* (New York: E. P. Dutton, 1897), 29–30.

72. Phillips Brooks, untitled poem [3], bMS AM 1594.2, (78).

73. Brooks, "Centralizing Power of the Gospel," 3.

74. Phillips Brooks, "Teaching Religion," *Essays and Addresses,* 60.

75. Phillips Brooks, "The Need of Enthusiasm for Humanity" address before the Evangelical Alliance, 1889, quoted in Allen, *Life and Letters,* 2:726.

Conclusion

1. Lewis Perry, *Boats against the Current: Revolution and Modernity, 1820–1869* (New York: Oxford University Press, 1993), 56.

2. James Brewer Stewart, "Boston, Abolition, and the Atlantic World, 1820–1861," in *Courage and Conscience: Black and White Abolitionists in Boston,* ed. Donald M. Jacobs (Bloomington: Indiana University Press, 1993), 116.

3. William G. Brooks, Sr., Diary, 1858–61, 642.

4. Stewart, "Boston, Abolition, and the Atlantic World," 118, 122–23.

5. Ibid., 114.

6. John Higham, *Writing American History: Essays on Modern Scholarship* (Bloomington: Indiana University Press, 1970), 190–91.

7. Allen, *Life and Letters,* 2:539.

8. Nordeau was only partly pessimistic; optimism appears in his espousal of the Zionist cause in the early twentieth century. Higham notes, however, the darkening influence on America of *Degeneration* (*Writing American History,* 91).

9. Higham remarks on Brooks Adams's "great conversion" from the despair of his *Law of Civilization and Decay* (1895) to an optimistic view of history in 1898, after which he appears to have made something of a nuisance of himself (*Writing American History,* 94).

10. A very different and more somber Stowe went on to write *Dred: A Tale of the Great Dismal Swamp* (Boston: Phillips, Sampson, 1856). See Sarah D. Hartshorne, "'Without Divine Intervention': Three Novels by 'Harriet Beecher Stowe Herself'" (Ph.D. diss., Brown University, 1990), 22–64.

11. See Gary Wills, *Lincoln at Gettysburg: The Words That Remade America* (New York: Simon and Schuster, 1992), esp. 101–11. Wills notes that Parker "contrasted the *ideal* Jesus with all the provisional expressions of that ideal in biblical texts or church doctrines" (108). Brooks, by contrast, made no such distinction between the "Transient and the Permanent in Christianity," to quote the title of Parker's famous essay (in *The Transcendentalists: An Anthology,* ed. Perry Miller [Cambridge: Harvard University Press, 1950], 259–83).

12. Wills, *Lincoln at Gettysburg,* 103.

13. Rose, *Victorian America,* 17.

14. That the celebration of Christmas was an issue between Anglicans and Congregationalists in New England is accurately and vividly portrayed in Harriet Beecher Stowe's *Poganuc People* (New York: Fords, Howard, and Hulbert, 1878), chaps. 1–3. Stowe also shows that writings of the church fathers were by no means the private domain of Episcopalians.

15. Robert Bruce Mullin, "Denominations as Bilingual Communities," in *Reimagining Denominationalism,* ed. Robert Bruce Mullin and Russell E. Richey (New York: Oxford University Press, 1994), 170.

16. See, for instance, Stout, *The New England Soul,* 228. See also Delattre, *Beauty and Sensibility,* 68–69; Conrad Cherry, *The Theology of Jonathan Edwards: A Reappraisal* (Garden City, N.Y.: Doubleday, 1966), 96–106; Robert W. Jensen, *America's Theologian: A Recommen-*

dation of Jonathan Edwards (New York: Oxford University Press, 1988), 115–22; Krister Sairsingh, "Jonathan Edwards and the Idea of Divine Glory: The Trinitarian Foundation of Edwards Theology and Its Ecclesial Import" (Ph.D. diss., Harvard University, 1986), 132–35. For the biblical background to Edwards's preaching, see David E. Laurence, "Religious Experience in the Biblical World of Jonathan Edwards: A Study in Eighteenth-Century Supernaturalism" (Ph.D. diss., Yale University, 1976).

17. "The purpose of art is to conceal artistry."

18. Phillips Brooks to William G. Brooks, Jr., 13 Jan. 1857, bMS AM 1594.1, (4), folder 1.

19. Phillips Brooks to C. A. L. Richards, 16 Feb. 1859, bMS AM 2022, (38). Gresley was curate of St. Chad's, Litchfield, and a Tractarian. See William T. Gresley, *Ecclesiastes Anglicanus: Being a Treatise on the Art of Preaching as Adapted to a Church of England Congregation* (London: Rivington, 1840 [1835]).

20. Phillips Brooks to Frederick Brooks, 3 Feb. 1859, bMS AM 1594.1, (5), folder 1.

21. Bolles, "Phillips Brooks," 1.

22. Hatch, *Democratization of American Christianity,* 14.

23. Joseph A. Conforti, "The Invention of the Great Awakening, 1795–1842," *Early American Literature* 26, no. 2 (1991), 99–117.

24. Allen C. Guelzo notes that "Episcopalian evangelicalism rose and fell almost exactly with the Whig party" ("A Test of Identity: The Vestments Controversy in the Reformed Episcopal Church, 1873–1897," *Anglican and Episcopal History* 61, no. 3 [Sept. 1992], 310).

25. Lears, *No Place of Grace,* 202.

26. Ferdinand Ewer, *Catholicity, Protestantism, and Romanism* (New York: G. P. Putnam's Sons, 1879), 296.

27. Yevgeny Yevtushenko, in "Early Illusions" (1963) writes: "you see, it is not the ability to be as wise as the serpent, / it is not the doubtful honor of experience, / but the ability to be enchanted by the world / that reveals to us the world that really is" (*The Collected Poems, 1952–1991,* ed. Albert C. Todd et al., trans. Tina Tupikana-Glaessner et al. [1963; New York: Henry Holt, 1991], 121).

28. Charles H. Hopkins, *The Rise of the Social Gospel in American Protestantism, 1865–1915* (New Haven: Yale University Press, 1940), 19.

29. Brooks's role in the Social Gospel, which at the time of his death was beginning to gain more adherents, needs to be reassessed.

30. Coleridge is quoted in Abrams, "Structure and Style," 218.

31. Woolverton, *Colonial Anglicanism,* 198–200. The comparison of Brooks with Whitefield has its limits. Whereas Whitefield was emotion-

al and self-promotional, Brooks avoided both theatricality in the pulpit and any reference in and out of it to either his trials or his achievements.

32. Lawrence, "History of Preaching," 3:1317. See also Robert T. Oliver, *History of Public Speaking in America* (Boston: Allyn and Bacon, 1965), 389.

33. Stowe is quoted in Annie Fields, *Life and Letters of Harriet Beecher Stowe* (Boston: Houghton, Mifflin, 1898), 392.

34. Lundin, *Culture of Interpretation,* 74.

35. Ibid., 237.

36. Ibid.

37. Ibid., 246.

Index

JOHN F. WOOLVERTON was educated at Groton School and Harvard University. In 1963 he received his Ph.D. from Columbia University, where he studied under Richard Hofstadter and under Robert T. Handy of Union Theological Seminary. Since 1977 he has been editor of the international journal *Anglican and Episcopal History*. He is the author of *Colonial Anglicanism in North America* (1984) and has contributed articles to a number of scholarly journals as well as the *Encyclopedia of the North American Colonies*, the *Dictionary of Virginia Biography*, and the *American National Dictionary*. He has taught at Virginia Theological Seminary, Woodstock College, the College of William and Mary, and most recently at the Episcopal Theological Seminary of the Southwest. He and his wife reside in Center Sandwich, New Hampshire.